SIR GAWAIN AND THE GREEN KNIGHT

SIR GAWAIN AND THE GREEN KNIGHT

A NEW VERSE TRANSLATION

SIMON ARMITAGE

W. W. NORTON & COMPANY

New York   London

Copyright © 2007 by Simon Armitage
First American edition 2007

Frontispiece © British Library Board. All rights reserved.
(Cotton Nero A.x (art.3) folio 95 (old ink numbering 91)

Middle English text of *Sir Gawain and the Green Knight* reprinted by permission
of Everyman's Library, an imprint of Alfred A. Knopf.
Copyright © Everyman's Library 1962.

For information about permission to reproduce selections from this book,
write to Permissions, W. W. Norton & Company, Inc., 500 Fifth Avenue,
New York, NY 10110

For information about special discounts for bulk purchases, please contact
W. W. Norton Special Sales at specialsales@wwnorton.com or 800-233-4830

Manufacturing by RR Donnelley, Harrisonburg, VA
Book design by JAM Design
Production manager: Anna Oler

Library of Congress Cataloging-in-Publication Data

Gawain and the Grene Knight. English & English (Middle English)
Sir Gawain and the Green Knight : a new verse translation / [translated by]
Simon Armitage. — 1st American ed.
p. cm.
Middle English text, parallel English translation.
ISBN 978-0-393-06048-5
1. Gawain (Legendary character)—Romances. 2. Knights and knighthood—Poetry.
3. Arthurian romances. I. Armitage, Simon, 1963– II. Title.
PR065.G3A328 2007
821.1—dc22   2007028520

W. W. Norton & Company, Inc.
500 Fifth Avenue, New York, N.Y. 10110
www.wwnorton.com

W. W. Norton & Company Ltd.
Castle House, 75/76 Wells Street, London W1T 3QT

1 2 3 4 5 6 7 8 9 0

CONTENTS

INTRODUCTION

We know next to nothing about the author of the poem that has come to be called *Sir Gawain and the Green Knight*. It was probably written around 1400. In the early seventeenth century the manuscript was recorded as belonging to a Yorkshireman, Henry Saville of Bank. It was later acquired by Sir Robert Cotton, whose collection also included the Lindisfarne Gospels and the only existing manuscript of *Beowulf*. The poem then lay dormant for over two hundred years, not coming to light until Queen Victoria was on the throne, thus leapfrogging the attentions of some of our greatest writers and critics. The manuscript, a small, unprepossessing thing, would fit comfortably into an average-size hand, were anyone actually allowed to touch it. Now referred to as Cotton Nero A.x., it is considered not only a most brilliant example of Middle English poetry but one of the jewels in the crown of English Literature, and sits in the British Library under conditions of high security and controlled humidity.

To cast eyes on the manuscript, or even to shuffle the unbound pages of the Early English Text Society's facsimile edition, is to be intrigued by the handwriting; stern, stylish letters, like crusading chess pieces, fall into orderly ranks along faintly ruled lines. But the man whose calligraphy we ponder, a jobbing scribe, probably, was not the author. The person who has become known as the *Gawain* poet remains as shadowy as the pages themselves. Among many other reasons, it is partly this anonymity that has made the poem so attractive to latter-day translators. The lack of authorship seems to serve as an invitation, opening up a space within the poem for a new writer to occupy. Its comparatively recent rediscovery acts as a further draw; if Milton or Pope had put their stamp on it, or if Dr. Johnson had offered an opinion, or if Keats or Coleridge or Wordsworth had drawn it into their orbit, such an invitation might now appear less forthcoming.

The diction of the original tells us that its author was, broadly speaking, a northerner. Or we might say a midlander. The linguistic epicenter is thought to be located somewhere between north Staffordshire and south Lancashire. Some researchers claim to have identified Swythamley Grange as the Castle of Hautdesert, or the jagged peaks of The Roaches as those "rughe knokled knarres with knorned stones," (2166). Lud's Church, a natural fissure in the rocks near the village of Flash, in Debyshire, has been proposed as the site of the Green Chapel. "Hit hade a hole on the ende and on ayther syde, / And overgrowen with gresse in glodes anywhere; / And al was holw inwith, nobot an olde cave / Or a crevisse of an olde cragge" (2180–2183). It may or may not be the place, but to stand in that mossy cleft that cannot have changed much over the centuries is to believe that the author had an actual landscape in mind when he conceived the poem, and lured his young protagonist into a northern region to legitimize his vocabulary and to make good use of his surrounding geography. A similar strategy has informed this translation; although my own part of England is separated from Lud's Church by the swollen uplands of The Peak District, coaxing Gawain and his poem back into the Pennines was always part of the plan.

Of course, to the trained medievalist the poem is perfectly readable in its original form; no translation necessary. And even for the nonspecialist, certain lines, such as, "Bot Arthure wolde not ete til al were served," (85), especially when placed within the context of the narrative, present little problem. Conversely, lines such as "Forthi, iwysse, bi yowre wylle, wende me bihoves," (1065) are incomprehensible to the general reader. But it is the lines that fall somewhere between those extremes—the majority of lines, in fact—which fascinate the most. They seem to make sense, though not quite. To the untrained eye, it is as if the poem is lying beneath a thin coat of ice, tantalizingly near yet frustratingly blurred. To a contemporary poet, one interested in narrative and form, the urge to blow a little warm breath across that layer of frosting eventually proved irresistible. And even more so to a northerner who not only recognizes plenty of the poem's dialect but who detects an echo of his own speech within the original. Words such as "bide" (wait), "nobut" (nothing but), "childer" (children), "layke" (play), "karp" (talk), "bout" (without), "brid" (bird), "sam" (gather up), and "barlay" (truce) are still in usage in these parts, though mainly (and sadly) among members of the older generation.

Not all poems are stories, but *Sir Gawain and the Green Knight* most certainly is. After briefly anchoring its historical credentials in the siege of Troy, the poem quickly delivers us into Arthurian Britain, at Christmastime, with the knights of the Round Table in good humor and full voice. But the festivities at Camelot are to be disrupted by the astonishing appearance of a green knight. Not just a knight wearing green clothes, but a weird being whose skin and hair is green, and whose horse is green as well. The gate-crasher lays down a seemingly absurd challenge, involving beheading and revenge. Alert to the opportunity, a young knight, Gawain, Arthur's nephew, rises from the table. What follows is a test of his courage and a test of his heart, and during the ensuing episodes, which span an entire calendar year, Gawain must steel himself against fear and temptation. The poem is also a ghost story, a thriller, a romance, an adventure story, and a morality tale. For want of a better word, it is also a myth, and like all great myths of the past its meanings seem to have adapted and evolved, proving itself eerily relevant six hundred years later. As one example, certain aspects of Gawain's situation seem oddly redolent of a more contemporary predicament, namely our complex and delicate relationship with the natural world. The *Gawain* poet had never heard of climate change and was not a prophet anticipating the onset of global warming. But medieval society lived hand in hand with nature, and nature was as much an enemy as a friend. It is not just for decoration that the poem includes passages relating to the turning of the seasons, or detailed accounts of the landscape, or graphic descriptions of our dealings with the animal kingdom. The knight who throws down the challenge at Camelot is both ghostly and real. Supernatural, yes, but also flesh and blood. He is something in the likeness of ourselves, and he is not purple or orange or blue with yellow stripes. Gawain must negotiate a deal with a man who wears the colors of the leaves and the fields. He must strike an honest bargain with this manifestation of nature, and his future depends on it.

Over the years there have been dozens, possibly hundreds of translations of *Sir Gawain and the Green Knight*, ranging from important scholarly restorations, to freehanded poetic or prose versions, to exercises in form and technique by students of Middle English, many of them posted on the Internet. Some translators, for perfectly valid reasons and with great success, have chosen not to imitate its highly alliterative form. But to me, alliteration is the warp and weft of the poem, without which it is just so many fine threads. In some very elemental way, the story and the sense of the poem is directly located within its sound. The percussive patterning of the words serves to reinforce their meaning and to countersink them within the memory. So in trying to harmonize with the original rather than transcribe every last word of it, certain liberties have been taken. This is not an exercise in linguistic forensics or medieval history; the intention has always been to produce a living, inclusive, and readable piece of work in its own right.

Readers of this parallel text edition are offered the opportunity of allowing their eye to travel across the gutter of the book from an original line to its corresponding translation. Occasionally they will be presented with something like a mirror image, or at least a striking resemblance. The first line of the poem, for example, aside for the odd bit of touching-up, is a fairly honest reproduction. Other lines, however, will be less recognizable in their altered state. There is plenty to argue with here, and for some commentators, this kind of approach will always be unacceptable. But this is a poem, not a crib or a glossary, and in imitating the alliterative style of *Sir Gawain and the Green Knight* it is inevitable that the translator will be led away from the words of the original and their direct contemporary equivalents. Take the much discussed issue of the *Gawain* poet's many words for "knight" or "man." Terms at his disposal included "freke," "hathel," "burne," "tulk," "segge," "schalk," and "gome." In a literal translation, with the use of a dictionary, each of those obsolete words could be replaced by a modern word of the same meaning, without too much agonizing over its acoustic properties or pronunciation. But in an alliterative translation those agonies must be experienced; in trawling for appropriate substitute words the net must be cast wider. In the "bob and wheel" sections where meter and rhyme also enter the equation, further deviations are inevitable. Lines 81–82 read: "The comlokest to discrye / Ther glent with yyen gray" (Broadly speaking, the fairest to behold / looked on with gray eyes). A literal translation gives us the cold facts of Guinevere's beauty, yet the unspoken poetic intelligence suggests that her eyes are precious stones, more priceless than the "best gemmes" mentioned in the previous line. Of all the jewels that surround her, it is her own eyes that glint and gleam the most. My own poetic response has been to introduce "quartz" and "queen," despite neither of those words being present in the original lines. I hope that readers will be able to see this as a kind of controlled and necessary flirtation, rather than carefree unfaithfulness or mindless infidelity.

Aside from the technical requirements of the poem, there are other reasons for departing from the literal, and those reasons are to do with the very nature of poetry itself. Poetry is not just meaning and information. Poetry is about manner as much as it is about matter—the manner in which words behave under certain conditions and in particular surroundings. Such behaviors give poems their unique character. Over time these behaviors change, or come to signify different things, and their latter-day counterparts are more likely to be found in the imagination than in the dictionary or the encyclopedia. For this reason the poet who works as a translator will rarely be content with a tit-for-tat exchange of one language into another, no matter how scrupulous the transfer. Here is line 1137:

By that any daylight lemed upon erthe

"By the time that some daylight shone upon earth" would be a reasonable literal translation. At first sight this not a particularly appealing line. To begin with, it is one of the moments in the poem when the alliteration falters. Also, for a description of the life-bringing dawn, and as a curtain-raiser to one of the greatest hunting scenes in all literature, it seems pretty tame. But there is power here, and much of that power is invested in that single word "lemed," from an Old Norse word, "ljóma," meaning "to shine." It is not a word used in English these days, which is a pity, because as a verb it has much to recommend it. The mouth opens to announce this word, and the tongue pushes forward, launching that first "l." Then something is projected outward, from the breathed "e" to the agreeable, humming "m," all the way through to that final "d," like a soft landing, the laying down of light "upon" the ground. If it is onomatopoeic it is also metaphorical, magical even, a one word image. It signals to me that poetry is at work here, and it seems to demand a poetic response. My own, "So as morning was lifting its lamp to the land" introduces words and concepts that are foreign to the original line, but not, I hope, out of keeping with its ambitions or intentions. Neither does it derail the story line or contradict the basic facts. Ornamentation has happened here, but hopefully the structural integrity has not been compromised.

Returning to the subject of alliteration, it should be mentioned that within each line it is the *stressed* syllables that count. A translated line like, "and retrieves the intestines in time-honored style," (1612) might appear not to alliterate at first glance. But read it out loud, and the repetition of that "t" sound—the tut-tutting, the spit of revulsion, the squirming of the warm, wet tongue as it makes contact with the roof of the mouth—seems to suggest a physical relationship with the action being described. If the technique is effective, as well as understanding what we are being told we take a step closer to actually experiencing it. It is an attempt to combine meaning with feeling. This is a translation not only for the eye, but for the ear and the voice as well. Further to that, it is worth noting that the pronunciation of our hero's very name is not universally agreed upon. To many he is *Ga*wain. The original author clearly alliterated on the "G," suggesting he also stressed the first syllable of the word. But there are other moments in the text, such as the perfectly iambic quatrain at 1948, where the rhythm suggests the opposite, as in Ga*wain,* which is the way I have always referred to him. For the convenience of having my cake and eating it, sometimes I have allowed the tough-looking "G" to perform a visual alliteration, and sometimes I have required the "w" to act as the load bearer.

Sir Gawain and the Green Knight is a poem that succeeds through a series of vivid contrasts: standard English contrasting with colloquial speech; the devotion and virtue of the young knight contrasting with the growling threats of his green foe; exchanges of courtly love contrasting with none-too-subtle sexual innuendo; exquisite robes and priceless crowns contrasting with spurting blood and the steaming organs of butchered deer; polite, indoor society contrasting with the untamed, unpredictable outdoors . . . and so on. Those contrasts stretch the imaginative universe of the poem and make it three dimensional. Without the space they open up, there would be no poem to speak of. The same contrasts can be observed in the form of the poem as well as its tone, with elements of order and disorder at work throughout, often operating simultaneously. On the side of order we have the carefully crafted form, the very particular number of verses, and the rhyme and rhythm of the bob and wheel sections. On the side of disorder we have the unequal line lengths, the variable verse lengths, and the wildly fluctuating pace of the story. Even the alliteration, a constant and insistent heartbeat for the most part, misses a beat every now and again and flatlines completely on at least one occasion. So within the strictures and confines of this very formal piece we detect a human presence, the *Gawain* poet, a disciplined craftsman who also liked to run risks and take liberties. He would appear to have set himself a series of rules, then consciously and conspicuously gone about bending them. As his translator, I hope to have been guided by his example.

—*Simon Armitage*

A NOTE ON MIDDLE ENGLISH METER

imon Armitage's introduction to his splendid translation of *Sir Gawain and the Green Knight* provides all the basic information a reader might need to appreciate this work. For those readers who wish to hear, and to read, the original text, a few words on the poem's meter might be useful.

Metrical practice is determined by the deeper music of a language. In Germanic languages, the tonic, or accented syllable, is usually the first syllable of a word. In romance languages, by contrast, the tonic syllable falls toward, or at the end, of words. Germanic poets therefore highlight the beginning of words with alliteration, whereas romance poets (e.g., French or Italian) highlight the end of words with rhyme.

Alliteration (from Latin *litera*, alphabetic letter) consists of the repetition of an initial consonant sound or consonant cluster in consecutive or closely positioned words. Anglo-Saxon is the earlier, purely Germanic form of English used in England from the time of the Germanic invasions in the fifth century until the Norman Conquest in 1066. All poetry in Anglo-Saxon is alliterative. Only after the Norman Conquest, and the impact of French, did poets writing in English begin to use rhyme as a fundamental part of their metrical practice. Anglo-Saxon poetry and metrical practice were for the most part displaced by models of continental poetry deploying rhyme, even if there are some very brilliant, post-Conquest exceptions (notably the alliterative Lawman's *Brut,* c. 1190). From the mid-fourteenth century, however, for reasons not fully understood, an extraordinary range of alliterative poems appear. It seems likely that this body of work constitutes a revival of an older metrical tradition. Poems written or somehow located in the west of England (naturally the most conservative linguistically, given the pressure for change from the east) from the middle of the fourteenth century use alliterative meter in a wide range of poetic genres. To this group of texts, and in particular to a more refined, technically disciplined metrical practice characteristic of North-Western texts, the remarkable *Sir Gawain and the Green Knight* belongs. For all his commitment to alliterative verse of great technical virtuosity, however, the *Gawain*-poet also signals that he's skilful in rhyme, too, since each stanza ends with five short rhyming lines.

The poem is written in stanzas. The number of lines per stanza varies. The line is longer, and does not contain a fixed number or pattern of stresses like the classical alliterative meter of Anglo-Saxon poetry. The standard metrical pattern is *a a/a x*, where *a* signifies an alliterating, stressed syllable; / signifies a caesura; and *x* signifies a nonalliterating stressed syllable. The poet frequently enriches this pattern. Each stanza closes, as mentioned above, with five short lines, rhyming *a b a b a*. The first of these rhyming lines contains just one stress, and is called the "bob"; the four three stress lines that follow are called the "wheel."

—*James Simpson*

SIR GAWAIN AND THE GREEN KNIGHT

I

Sithen the sege and the assaut was sesed at Troye,
The borgh brittened and brent to brondes and askes,
The tulk that the trammes of tresoun ther wroght
Was tried for his tricherie, the trewest on erthe.
Hit was Ennias the athel and his highe kynde
That sithen depreced provinces, and patrounes bicome
Welneghe of al the wele in the West Iles:
Fro riche Romulus to Rome ricchis hym swythe,
With gret bobbaunce that burghe he biges upon fyrst,
10   And nevenes hit his aune nome, as hit now hat;
Ticius to Tuskan, and teldes bigynnes;
Langaberde in Lumbardie lyftes up homes;
And fer over the French flod Felix Brutus
On mony bonkkes ful brode Bretayn he settes
    wyth wynne,
   Where werre and wrake and wonder
   Bi sythes has wont therinne,
   And oft bothe blysse and blunder
   Ful skete has skyfted synne.

20   Ande quen this Bretayn was bigged bi this burn rych,
Bolde bredden therinne, baret that lofden,
In mony turned tyme tene that wroghten.
Mo ferlyes on this folde han fallen here oft

FITT I

Once the siege and assault of Troy had ceased,
with the city a smoke-heap of cinders and ash,
the traitor who contrived such betrayal there
was tried for his treachery, the truest on earth;
so Aeneas, it was, with his noble warriors
went conquering abroad, laying claim to the crowns
of the wealthiest kingdoms in the western world.
Mighty Romulus quickly careered towards Rome
and conceived a city in magnificent style
which from then until now has been known by his name.
Ticius constructed townships in Tuscany
and Langobard did likewise building homes in Lombardy.
And further afield, over the Sea of France,
on Britain's broad hilltops, Felix Brutus made
    his stand.
   And wonder, dread and war
   have lingered in that land
   where loss and love in turn
   have held the upper hand.

After Britain was built by this founding father
a bold race bred there, battle-happy men
causing trouble and torment in turbulent times,
and through history more strangeness has happened here

Then in any other that I wot, syn that ilk tyme.

Bot of alle that here bult of Bretaygne kynges

Ay was Arthur the hendest, as I haf herde telle.

Forthi an aunter in erde I attle to schawe,

That a selly in sight summe men hit holden,

And an outtrage awenture of Arthures wonderes.

30 If ye wyl lysten this laye bot on littel quile,

I schal telle hit astit, as I in toun herde,

with tonge;

As hit is stad and stoken

In stori stif and stronge,

With lel letteres loken,

In londe so has ben longe.

This kyng lay at Camylot upon Krystmasse

With mony luflych lorde, ledes of the best,

Rekenly of the Rounde Table alle tho rich brether,

40 With rych revel oryght and rechles merthes.

Ther tournayed tulkes by tymes ful mony,

Justed ful jolilé thise gentyle knightes,

Sythen kayred to the court, caroles to make.

For ther the fest was ilyche ful fiften dayes,

With alle the mete and the mirthe that men couthe avyse:

Such glaum ande gle glorious to here,

Dere dyn upon day, daunsyng on nyghtes;

Al was hap upon heghe in halles and chambres

With lordes and ladies, as levest him thoght.

50 With all the wele of the worlde thay woned ther samen,

The most kyd knyghtes under Krystes selven,

And the lovelokkest ladies that ever lif haden,

And he the comlokest kyng that the court haldes.

than anywhere else I know of on Earth.
But most regal of rulers in the royal line
was Arthur, who I heard is honored above all,
and the inspiring story I intend to spin
has moved the hearts and minds of many—
an awesome episode in the legends of Arthur.
30 So listen a little while to my tale if you will
and I'll tell it as it's told in the town where it trips from
                    the tongue;
            and as it has been inked
            in stories bold and strong,
            through letters which, once linked,
            have lasted loud and long.

It was Christmas at Camelot—King Arthur's court,
where the great and the good of the land had gathered,
all the righteous lords of the ranks of the Round Table
40 quite properly carousing and reveling in pleasure.
Time after time, in tournaments of joust,
they had lunged at each other with leveled lances
then returned to the castle to carry on their caroling,
for the feasting lasted a full fortnight and one day,
with more food and drink than a fellow could dream of.
The hubbub of their humor was heavenly to hear:
pleasant dialogue by day and dancing after dusk,
so the house and its hall were lit with happiness
and lords and ladies were luminous with joy.
50 Such a coming together of the gracious and the glad:
the most chivalrous and courteous knights known to Christendom;
the most wonderful women to have walked in this world;
the handsomest king to be crowned at court.

For al was this fayre folk in her first age
                    on sille,
          The hapnest under heven,
          Kyng hyghest mon of wylle;
          Hit were now gret nye to neven
          So hardy a here on hille.

60   Wyle Nw Yer was so yep that hit was nwe cummen,
     That day doubble on the dece was the douth served,
     Fro the kyng was cummen with knyghtes into the halle,
     The chauntré of the chapel cheved to an ende.
     Loude crye was ther kest of clerkes and other,
     Nowel nayted onewe, nevened ful ofte;
     And sythen riche forth runnen to reche hondeselle,
     Yeyed yeres yiftes on high, yelde hem bi hond,
     Debated busyly aboute tho giftes.
     Ladies laghed ful loude, thogh thay lost haden,
70   And he that wan was not wrothe, that may ye wel trawe.
     Alle this mirthe thay maden to the mete tyme.
     When thay had waschen worthyly thay wenten to sete,
     The best burne ay abof, as hit best semed;
     Whene Guenore, ful gay, graythed in the myddes,
     Dressed on the dere des, dubbed al aboute—
     Smal sendal bisides, a selure hir over
     Of tryed Tolouse, of Tars tapites innoghe,
     That were enbrawded and beten wyth the best gemmes
     That myght be preved of prys wyth penyes to bye
80   in daye.
          The comlokest to discrye
          Ther glent with yyen gray;
          A semloker that ever he syye,
          Soth moght no mon say.

Fine folk with their futures before them, there in
        that hall.
      Their highly honored king
      was happiest of all:
      no nobler knights had come
      within a castle's wall.

60   With New Year so young it still yawned and stretched
helpings were doubled on the dais that day.
And as king and company were coming to the hall
the choir in the chapel fell suddenly quiet,
then a chorus erupted from the courtiers and clerks:
"Noel," they cheered, then "Noel, Noel,"
"New Year Gifts!" the knights cried next
as they pressed forwards to offer their presents,
teasing with frivolous favors and forfeits,
till those ladies who lost couldn't help but laugh,
70 and the undefeated were far from forlorn.
Their merrymaking rolled on in this manner until mealtime,
when, washed and worthy, they went to the table,
and were seated in order of honor, as was apt,
with Guinevere in their gathering, gloriously framed
at her place on the platform, pricelessly curtained
by silk to each side, and canopied across
with French weave and fine tapestry from the far east
studded with stones and stunning gems.
Pearls beyond pocket. Pearls beyond purchase
80   or price.
      But not one stone outshone
      the quartz of the queen's eyes;
      with hand on heart, no one
      could argue otherwise.

Bot Arthure wolde not ete til al were served,

He was so joly of his joyfnes, and sumquat childgered:

His lif liked hym lyght, he lovied the lasse

Auther to longe lye or to longe sitte,

So bisied him his yonge blod and his brayn wylde.

90 And also another maner meved him eke,

That he thurgh nobelay had nomen he wolde never ete

Upon such a dere day, er hym devised were

Of sum aventurus thyng an uncouthe tale,

Of sum mayn mervayle, that he myght trawe,

Of alderes, of armes, of other aventurus;

Other sum segg hym bisoght of sum siker knyght

To joyne wyth hym in justyng, in jopardé to lay,

Lede lif for lyf, leve uchon other,

As fortune wolde fulsun hom, the fayrer to have.

100 This was kynges countenaunce where he in court were,

At uch farand fest among his fre meny

in halle.

Therfore of face so fere

He stightles stif in stalle;

Ful yep in that Nw Yere,

Much mirthe he mas with alle.

Thus ther stondes in stale the stif kyng hisselven,

Talkkande bifore the hyghe table of trifles ful hende.

There gode Gawan was graythed Gwenore bisyde,

110 And Agravayn a la dure mayn on that other syde sittes,

Bothe the kynges sister sunes and ful siker knightes;

Bischop Bawdewyn abof bigines the table,

And Ywan, Uryn son, ette with hymselven.

Thise were dight on the des and derworthly served,

And sithen mony siker segge at the sidbordes.

But Arthur would not eat until all were served.
He brimmed with ebullience, being almost boyish
in his love of life, and what he liked the least
was to sit still watching the seasons slip by.
His blood was busy and he buzzed with thoughts,
90 and the matter which played on his mind at that moment
was his pledge to take no portion from his plate
on such a special day until a story was told:
some far-fetched yarn or outrageous fable,
the tallest of tales, yet one ringing with truth,
like the action-packed epics of men-at-arms.
Or till some chancer had challenged his chosen knight,
dared him, with a lance, to lay life on the line,
to stare death face-to-face and accept defeat
should fortune or fate smile more favorably on his foe.
100 Within Camelot's castle this was the custom,
and at feasts and festivals when the fellowship
                 would meet.
            With features proud and fine
            he stood there tall and straight,
            a king at Christmastime
            amid great merriment.

And still he stands there just being himself,
chatting away charmingly, exchanging views.
Good Sir Gawain is seated by Guinevere,
110 and at Arthur's other side sits Agravain the Hard Hand,
both nephews of the king and notable knights.
At the head sat Bishop Baldwin as Arthur's guest of honor,
with Ywain, son of Urien, to eat beside him.
And as soon as the nobles had sampled the spread
the stalwarts on the benches to both sides were served.

Then the first cors come with crakkyng of trumpes,
Wyth mony baner ful bryght that therbi henged;
Nwe nakryn noyse with the noble pipes,
Wylde werbles and wyght wakned lote,
120   That mony hert ful highe hef at her towches.
Dayntés dryven therwyth of ful dere metes,
Foysoun of the fresche, and on so fele disches
That pine to fynde the place the peple biforne
For to sette the sylveren that sere sewes halden
                     on clothe.
              Iche lede as he loved hymselve
              Ther laght withouten lothe;
              Ay two had disches twelve,
              Good ber and bryght wyn bothe.

130   Now wyl I of hor servise say yow no more,
For uch wyye may wel wit no wont that ther were.
An other noyse ful newe neghed bilive,
That the lude myght haf leve liflode to cach.
For unethe was the noyce not a whyle sesed,
And the fyrst cource in the court kyndely served,
Ther hales in at the halle dor an aghlich mayster,
On the most on the molde on mesure hyghe,
Fro the swyre to the swange so sware and so thik,
And his lyndes and his lymes so longe and so grete,
140   Half etayn in erde I hope that he were;
Bot mon most I algate mynn hym to bene,
And that the myriest in his muckel that myght ride,
For of bak and of brest al were his bodi sturne,
Both his wombe and his wast were worthily smale,
And alle his fetures folwande in forme that he hade,
                     ful clene.

The first course comes in to the fanfare and clamor
of blasting trumpets hung with trembling banners,
then pounding double-drums and dinning pipes,
weird sounds and wails of such warbled wildness
120   that to hear and feel them made the heart float free.
Flavorsome delicacies of flesh were fetched in
and the freshest of foods, so many in fact
there was scarcely space to present the stews
or to set the soups in the silver bowls on
              the cloth.
          Each guest received his share
          of bread or meat or broth;
          a dozen plates per pair—
          plus beer or wine, or both!

130   Now, on the subject of supper I'll say no more
as it's obvious to everyone that no one went without.
Because another sound, a new sound, suddenly drew near,
which might signal the king to sample his supper,
for barely had the horns finished blowing their breath
and with starters just spooned to the seated guests,
a fearful form appeared, framed in the door:
a mountain of a man, immeasurably high,
a hulk of a human from head to hips,
so long and thick in his loins and his limbs
140   I should genuinely judge him to be a half giant,
or a most massive man, the mightiest of mortals.
But handsome, too, like any horseman worth his horse,
for despite the bulk and brawn of his body
his stomach and waist were slender and sleek.
In fact in all features he was finely formed
              it seemed.

For wonder of his hwe men hade,

Set in his semblaunt sene;

He ferde as freke were fade,

150 And overal enker grene.

Ande al graythed in grene this gome and his wedes:

A strayt cote ful streght that stek on his sides,

A mere mantile abof, mensked withinne

With pelure pured apert, the pane ful clene

With blythe blaunner ful bryght, and his hod bothe,

That was laght fro his lokkes and layde on his schulderes;

Heme, wel-haled hose of that same grene,

That spenet on his sparlyr, and clene spures under

Of bryght golde, upon silk bordes barred ful ryche,

160 And scholes under schankes there the schalk rides.

And alle his vesture verayly was clene verdure,

Bothe the barres of his belt and other blythe stones,

That were richely rayled in his aray clene

Aboutte hymself and his sadel, upon silk werkes,

That were to tor for to telle of tryfles the halve

That were enbrauded abof, wyth bryddes and flyyes,

With gay gaudi of grene, the golde ay inmyddes.

The pendauntes of his payttrure, the proude cropure,

His molaynes and alle the metail anamayld was thenne;

170 The steropes that he stod on stayned of the same,

And his arsouns al after and his athel skurtes,

That ever glemered and glent al of grene stones.

The fole that he ferkkes on fyn of that ilke,

sertayn:

A grene hors gret and thikke,

A stede ful stif to strayne,

Amazement seized their minds,
no soul had ever seen
a knight of such a kind—
150   entirely emerald green.

And his gear and garments were green as well:
a tight fitting tunic, tailored to his torso,
and a cloak to cover him, the cloth fully lined
with smoothly shorn fur clearly showing, and faced
with all-white ermine, as was the hood,
worn shawled on his shoulders, shucked from his head.
On his lower limbs his leggings were also green,
wrapped closely round his calves, and his sparkling spurs
were green-gold, strapped with stripy silk,
160 and were set on his stockings, for this stranger was shoeless.
In all vestments he revealed himself veritably verdant!
From his belt hooks and buckle to the baubles and gems
arrayed so richly around his costume
and adorning the saddle, stitched onto silk.
All the details of his dress are difficult to describe,
embroidered as it was with butterflies and birds,
green beads emblazoned on a background of gold.
All the horse's tack—harness strap, hind strap,
the eye of the bit, each alloy and enamel
170 and the stirrups he stood in were similarly tinted,
and the same with the cantle and the skirts of the saddle,
all glimmering and glinting with the greenest jewels.
And the horse: every hair was green, from hoof
       to mane.
   A steed of pure green stock.
   Each snort and shudder strained

In brawden brydel quik—

To the gome he was ful gayn.

Wel gay was this gome gered in grene,

180 And the here of his hed of his hors swete.

Fayre fannand fax umbefoldes his schulderes;

A much berd as a busk over his brest henges,

That wyth his highlich here that of his hed reches

Was evesed al umbetorne abof his elbowes,

That half his armes therunder were halched in the wyse

Of a kynges capados that closes his swyre.

The mane of that mayn hors much to hit lyke,

Wel cresped and cemmed, wyth knottes ful mony

Folden in wyth fildore aboute the fayre grene,

190 Ay a herle of the here, an other of golde.

The tayl and his toppyng twynnen of a sute,

And bounden bothe wyth a bande of a bryght grene,

Dubbed wyth ful dere stones, as the dok lasted;

Sythen thrawen wyth a thwong, a thwarle-knot alofte,

Ther mony belles ful bryght of brende golde rungen.

Such a fole upon folde, ne freke that hym rydes,

Was never sene in that sale wyth syght er that tyme,

with yye.

He loked as layt so lyght,

200   So sayd al that hym syye;

Hit semed as no mon myght

Under his dynttes dryye.

Whether hade he no helme ne hawbergh nauther,

Ne no pysan, ne no plate that pented to armes,

Ne no schafte, ne no schelde, to schwve ne to smyte,

Bot in his on honde he hade a holyn bobbe,

the hand-stitched bridle, but
his rider had him reined.

The fellow in green was in fine fettle.
180 The hair of his head was as green as his horse,
fine flowing locks which fanned across his back,
plus a bushy green beard growing down to his breast,
and his face hair along with the hair of his head
was lopped in a line at elbow length
so half his arms were gowned in green growth,
crimped at the collar, like a king's cape.
The mane of his mount was groomed to match,
combed and knotted into curlicues
then tinseled with gold, tied and twisted
190 green over gold, green over gold. . . .
The fetlocks were finished in the same fashion
with bright green ribbon braided with beads,
as was the tail—to its tippety-tip!
And a long, tied thong lacing it tight
was strung with gold bells which resounded and shone.
No waking man had witnessed such a warrior
or weird warhorse—otherworldly, yet flesh
                    and bone.
            A look of lightning flashed
200   from somewhere in his soul.
            The force of that man's fist
            would be a thunderbolt.

Yet he wore no helmet and no hauberk either,
no armored apparel or plate was apparent,
and he swung no sword nor sported any shield,
but held in one hand a sprig of holly—

That is grattest in grene when greves ar bare,
And an ax in his other, a hoge and unmete,
A spetos sparthe to expoun in spelle, quo-so myght.
210 The hede of an elnyerde the large lenkthe hade,
The grayn al of grene stele and of golde hewen,
The bit burnyst bryght, with a brod egge
As wel schapen to schere as scharp rasores.
The stele of a stif staf the sturne hit bi grypte,
That was wounden wyth yrn to the wandes ende,
And al bigraven with grene in gracios werkes;
A lace lapped aboute, that louked at the hede,
And so after the halme halched ful ofte,
Wyth tryed tasseles therto tacched innoghe
220 On botouns of the bryght grene brayden ful ryche.
This hathel heldes hym in and the halle entres,
Drivande to the heghe dece, dut he no wothe.
Haylsed he never one, bot heghe he over loked.
The fyrst word that he warp: "Wher is," he sayd,
"The governour of this gyng? Gladly I wolde
Se that segg in syght, and with hymself speke
        raysoun."
         To knyghtes he kest his yye,
         And reled hym up and doun,
230   He stemmed and con studie
         Quo walt ther most renoun.

Ther was lokyng on lenthe, the lude to beholde,
For uch mon had mervayle quat hit mene myght
That a hathel and a horse myght such a hwe lach
As growe grene as the gres and grener hit semed,
Then grene aumayl on golde glowande bryghter.
Al studied that ther stod, and stalked hym nerre,

of all the evergreens the greenest ever—
and in the other hand held the mother of all axes,
a cruel piece of kit I kid you not:
210 the head was an ell in length at least
and forged in green steel with a gilt finish;
the skull-busting blade was so stropped and buffed
it could shear a man's scalp and shave him to boot.
The handle which fitted that fiend's great fist
was inlaid with iron, end to end,
with green pigment picking out impressive designs.
From stock to neck, where it stopped with a knot,
a lace was looped the length of the haft,
trimmed with tassels and tails of string
220 fastened firmly in place by forest-green buttons.
And he kicks on, canters through that crowded hall
towards the top table, not the least bit timid,
cocksure of himself, sitting high in the saddle.
"And who," he bellows, without breaking breath,
"is governor of this gaggle? I'll be glad to know.
It's with him and him alone that I'll have
                    my say."
                The green man steered his gaze
                deep into every eye,
230   explored each person's face
                to probe for a reply.

The guests looked on. They gaped and they gawked
and were mute with amazement: what did it mean
that human and horse could develop this hue,
should grow to be grass-green or greener still,
like green enamel emboldened by bright gold?
Some stood and stared then stepped a little closer,

Wyth al the wonder of the worlde what he worch schulde.

For fele sellyes had thay sen, bot such never are;

240 Forthi for fantoum and fayryye the folk there hit demed.

Therfore to answare was arwe mony athel freke,

And al stouned at his steven and stonstil seten

In a swoghe sylence thurgh the sale riche:

As al were slypped upon slepe so slaked hor lotes

in hyye.

I deme hit not al for doute,

Bot sum for cortaysye;

Bot let hym that al schulde loute

Cast unto that wyye.

250 Thenn Arthour bifore the high dece that aventure byholdes,

And rekenly hym reverenced, for rad was he never,

And sayde: "Wyye, welcum iwys to this place,

The hede of this ostel Arthour I hat.

Light luflych adoun and lenge, I the praye,

And quat-so thy wylle is we schal wyt after."

"Nay, as help me," quoth the hathel, "he that on hyghe syttes,

To wone any quyle in this won, hit was not myn ernde.

Bot for the los of the, lede, is lyft up so hyghe,

And thy burgh and thy burnes best ar holden,

260 Stifest under stel-gere on stedes to ryde,

The wyghtest and the worthyest of the worldes kynde,

Preve for to play wyth in other pure laykes,

And here is kydde cortaysye, as I haf herd carp,

And that has wayned me hider, iwyis, at this tyme.

Ye may be seker bi this braunch that I bere here

That I passe as in pes, and no plyght seche.

For had I founded in fere, in feghtyng wyse,

I have a hauberghe at home and a helme bothe,

drawn near to the knight to know his next move;
they'd seen some sights, but this was something special,
240 a miracle or magic, or so they imagined.
Yet several of the lords were like statues in their seats,
left speechless and rigid, not risking a response.
The hall fell hushed, as if all who were present
had slipped into sleep or some trancelike state.

        No doubt

     not all were stunned and stilled

     by dread, but duty bound

     to hold their tongues until

     their sovereign could respond.

250 Then the king acknowledged this curious occurrence,
cordially addressed him, keeping his cool.
"A warm welcome, sir, this winter's night.
My name is Arthur, I am head of this house.
Won't you slide from that saddle and stay awhile,
and the business which brings you we shall learn of later."
"No," said the knight, "it's not in my nature
to idle or allack about this evening.
But because your acclaim is so loudly chorused,
and your castle and brotherhood are called the best,
260 the strongest men to ever mount the saddle,
the worthiest knights ever known to the world,
both in competition and true combat,
and since courtesy, so it's said, is championed here,
I'm intrigued, and attracted to your door at this time.
Be assured by this hollin stem here in my hand
that I mean no menace. So expect no malice,
for if I'd slogged here tonight to slay and slaughter
my helmet and hauberk wouldn't be at home

A schelde and a scharp spere, schinande bryght,
270   Ande other weppenes to welde, I wene wel, als;
Bot for I wolde no were, my wedes ar softer.
Bot if thou be so bold as alle burnes tellen,
Thou wyl grant me godly the gomen that I ask
                    bi ryght."
              Arthour con onsware,
              And sayd: "Sir cortays knyght,
              If thou crave batayl bare,
              Here fayles thou not to fyght."

"Nay, frayst I no fyght, in fayth I the telle.
280   Hit arn aboute on this bench bot berdles chylder;
If I were hasped in armes on a heghe stede,
Here is no mon me to mach, for myghtes so wayke.
Forthy I crave in this court a Crystemas gomen,
For hit is Yol and Nwe Yer, and here ar yep mony.
If any so hardy in this hou holdes hymselven,
Be so bolde in his blod, brayn in hys hede,
That dar stifly strike a strok for an other,
I schal gif hym of my gyft thys giserne ryche,
This ax, that is hevé innogh, to hondele as hym lykes,
290   And I schal bide the fyrst bur, as bare as I sitte.
If any freke be so felle to fonde that I telle,
Lepe lyghtly me to, and lach this weppen—
I quit-clayme hit for ever, kepe hit as his auen.
And I schal stonde hym a strok, stif on this flet,
Elles thou wyl dight me the dom to dele hym an other,
                    barlay;
              And yet gif hym respite
              A twelmonyth and a day.

and my sword and spear would be here at my side,
270 and more weapons of war, as I'm sure you're aware;
I'm clothed for peace, not kitted out for conflict.
But if you're half as honorable as I've heard folk say
you'll gracefully grant me this game which I ask for
                      by right."
              Then Arthur answered, "Knight
              most courteous, you claim
              a fair, unarmored fight.
              We'll see you have the same."

"I'm spoiling for no scrap, I swear. Besides,
280 the bodies on these benches are just bum-fluffed bairns.
If I'd ridden to your castle rigged out for a ruck
these lightweight adolescents wouldn't last a minute.
But it's Yuletide—a time of youthfulness, yes?
So at Christmas in this court I lay down a challenge:
if a person here present, within these premises,
is big or bold or red blooded enough
to strike me one stroke and be struck in return,
I shall give him as a gift this gigantic cleaver
and the axe shall be his to handle how he likes.
290 I'll kneel, bare my neck and take the first knock.
So who has the gall? The gumption? The guts?
Who'll spring from his seat and snatch this weapon?
I offer the axe—who'll have it as his own?
I'll afford one free hit from which I won't flinch,
and promise that twelve months will pass in peace,
                      then claim
              the duty I deserve
              in one year and one day.

Now hyye, and let se tite

Dar any herinne oght say."

If he hem stowned upon fyrst, stiller were thanne

Alle the heredmen in halle, the hygh and the lowe.

The renk on his rouncé hym ruched in his sadel,

And runischly his rede yyen he reled aboute,

Bende his bresed browes, blycande grene,

Wayved his berde for to wayte quo-so wolde ryse.

When non wolde kepe hym with carp he coghed ful hyghe,

Ande rimed hym ful richly, and ryght hym to speke:

"What, is this Arthures hous," quoth the hathel thenne,

"That al the rous rennes of thurgh ryalmes so mony?

Where is now your sourquydrye and your conquestes,

Your gryndellayk and your greme and your grete wordes?

Now is the revel and the renoun of the Rounde Table

Overwalt wyth a worde of on wyyes speche,

For al dares for drede withoute dynt schewed!"

Wyth this he laghes so loude that the lorde greved;

The blod schot for scham into his schyre face

and lere.

He wex as wroth as wynde;

So did alle that ther were.

The kyng, as kene bi kynde,

Then stod that stif mon nere.

Ande sayde: "Hathel, by heven thyn askyng is nys,

And as thou foly has frayst, fynde the behoves.

I know no gome that is gast of thy grete wordes.

Gif me now thy geserne, upon Godes halve,

And I schal baythen thy bone that thou boden habbes."

Lyghtly lepes he hym to, and laght at his honde;

Does no one have the nerve

to wager in this way?"

Flustered at first, now totally foxed

were the household and the lords, both the highborn and the low.

Still stirruped, the knight swiveled round in his saddle

looking left and right, his red eyes rolling

beneath the bristles of his bushy green brows,

his beard swishing from side to side.

When the court kept its counsel he cleared his throat

and stiffened his spine. Then he spoke his mind:

"So here is the House of Arthur," he scoffed,

310   "whose virtues reverberate across vast realms.

Where's the fortitude and fearlessness you're so famous for?

And the breathtaking bravery and the big-mouth bragging?

The towering reputation of the Round Table,

skittled and scuppered by a stranger—what a scandal!

You flap and you flinch and I've not raised a finger!"

Then he laughed so loud that their leader saw red.

Blood flowed to his fine-featured face and he raged

                    inside.

          His men were also hurt—

320   those words had pricked their pride.

          But born so brave at heart

          the king stepped up one stride.

"Your request," he countered, "is quite insane,

and folly finds the man who flirts with the fool.

No warrior worth his salt would be worried by your words,

so in heaven's good name hand over the axe

and I'll happily fulfil the favor you ask."

He strides to him swiftly and seizes his arm;

Then feersly that other freke upon fote lyghtis.

330 Now has Arthure his axe, and the halme grypes,
And sturnely stures hit aboute, that stryke wyth hit thoght.
The stif mon hym bifore stod upon hyght,
Herre then ani in the hous by the hede and more.
Wyth sturne schere ther he stod he stroked his berde,
And wyth a countenaunce dryye he drow doun his cote,
No more mate ne dismayd for hys mayn dintes
Then any burne upon bench hade broght hym to drynk
        of wyne.
        Gawan, that sate bi the quene,
340   To the kyng he can enclyne:
        "I beseche now with sawes sene
        This melly mot be myne."

"Wolde ye, worthilych lorde," quoth Wawan to the kyng,
"Bid me bowe fro this benche and stonde by yow there,
That I wythoute vylanye myght voyde this table,
And that my legge lady lyked not ille,
I wolde com to your counseyl bifore your cort ryche.
For me think hit not semly, as hit is soth knawen,
Ther such an askyng is hevened so hyghe in your sale,
350 Thagh ye yourself be talenttyf, to take hit to yourselven,
Whil mony so bolde yow aboute upon bench sytten,
That under heven, I hope, non hagherer of wylle,
Ne better bodyes on bent ther baret is rered.
I am the wakkest, I wot, and of wyt feblest,
And lest lur of my lyf, quo laytes the sothe.
Bot for as much as ye ar myn em, I am only to prayse:
No bounté bot your blod I in my bodé knowe.
And sythen this note is so nys that noght hit yow falles,
And I have frayned hit at yow fyrst, foldes hit to me;

the man-mountain dismounts in one mighty leap.

330 Then Arthur grips the axe, grabs it by its haft

and takes it above him, intending to attack.

Yet the stranger before him stands up straight,

highest in the house by at least a head.

Quite simply he stands there stroking his beard,

fiddling with his coat, his face without fear,

about to be bludgeoned, but no more bothered

than a guest at the table being given a goblet

                  of wine.

           By Guinevere, Gawain

340   now to his king inclines

           and says, "I stake my claim.

           This moment must be mine."

"Should you call me, courteous lord," said Gawain to his king,

"to rise from my seat and stand at your side,

politely take leave of my place at the table

and quit without causing offence to my queen,

then I shall come to your counsel before this great court.

For I find it unfitting, as my fellow knights would,

when a deed of such daring is dangled before us

350 that you take on this trial—tempted as you are—

when brave, bold men are seated on these benches,

men never matched in the mettle of their minds,

never beaten or bettered in the field of battle.

I am weakest of your warriors and feeblest of wit;

loss of my life would be grieved the least.

Were I not your nephew my life would mean nothing;

to be born of your blood is my body's only claim.

Such a foolish affair is unfitting for a king,

so, being first to come forward, it should fall to me.

360 And if I carp not comlyly, let alle this cort rych
　　　　bout blame."
　　　Ryche togeder con roun,
　　　And sythen thay redden alle same
　　　To ryd the kyng wyth croun,
　　　And gif Gawan the game.

　　Then comaunded the kyng the knyght for to ryse,
　　And he ful radly up ros and ruchched hym fayre,
　　Kneled doun bifore the kyng, and caches that weppen;
　　And he luflyly hit hym laft, and lyfte up his honde
370 And gef hym Goddes blessyng, and gladly hym biddes
　　That his hert and his honde schulde hardi be bothe.
　　"Kepe the, cosyn," quoth the kyng, "that thou on kyrf sette,
　　And if thou redes hym ryght, redly I trowe
　　That thou schal byden the bur that he schal bede after."
　　Gawan gos to the gome, with giserne in honde,
　　And he baldly hym bydes, he bayst never the helder.
　　Then carppes to Sir Gawan the knyght in the grene:
　　"Refourme we oure forwardes, er we fyrre passe.
　　Fyrst I ethe the, hathel, how that thou hattes,
380 That thou me telle truly, as I tryst may."
　　"In god fayth," quoth the goode knyght, "Gawan I hatte,
　　That bede the this buffet, quat-so bifalles after,
　　And at this tyme twelmonyth take at the another
　　Wyth what weppen so thou wylt, and wyth no wyy elles
　　　　　on lyve."
　　　That other onswares agayn:
　　　"Sir Gawan, so mot I thryve,
　　　As I am ferly fayn
　　　This dint that thou schal dryve."

360   And if my proposal is improper, let no other person
                          stand blame."
                    The knighthood then unites
                    and each knight says the same:
                    their king can stand aside
                    and give Gawain the game.

      So the sovereign instructed his knight to stand.
      Getting to his feet he moved graciously forward
      and knelt before Arthur, taking hold of the axe.
      Letting go of it, Arthur then held up his hand
370   to give young Gawain the blessing of God
      and hope he finds firmness in heart and fist.
      "Take care, young cousin, to catch him cleanly,
      use full-blooded force then you needn't fear
      the blow which he threatens to trade in return."
      Gawain, with the weapon, walked towards the warrior,
      and they stood face-to-face, not one man afraid.
      Then the green knight spoke, growled at Gawain:
      "Before we compete, repeat what we've promised.
      And start by saying your name to me, sir,
380   and tell me the truth so I can take it on trust."
      "In good faith, it's Gawain," said the God-fearing knight,
      "I heave this axe, and whatever happens after,
      in twelvemonth's time I'll be struck in return
      with any weapon you wish, and by you and you
                          alone."
                    The other answers, says
                    "Well, by my living bones,
                    I welcome you Gawain
                    to bring the blade-head home."

390 "Bi gog," quoth the grene knyght, "Sir Gawan, me lykes
That I schal fange at thy fust that I haf frayst here.
And thou has redily rehersed, bi resoun ful trwe,
Clanly al the covenaunt that I the kynge asked,
Saf that thou schal siker me, segge, bi thi trawthe,
That thou schal seche me thiself, where-so thou hopes
I may be funde upon folde, and foch the such wages
As thou deles me to-day bifore this douthe ryche."
"Where schulde I wale the," quoth Gauan, "where is thy place?
I wot never where thou wonyes, bi hym that me wroght,
400 Ne I know not the, knyght, thy cort ne thi name.
Bot teche me truly therto, and telle me howe thou hattes,
And I schal ware alle my wyt to wynne me theder;
And that I swere the for sothe, and by my seker traweth."
"That is innogh in Nwe Yer, hit nedes no more,"
Quoth the gome in the grene to Gawan the hende:
"Yif I the telle trwly, quen I the tape have
And thou me smothely has smyten, smartly I the teche
Of my hous and my home and myn owen nome.
Then may thou frayst my fare, and forwardes holde;
410 And if I spende no speche, thenne spedes thou the better,
For thou may leng in thy londe and layt no fyrre—
                    bot slokes!
            Ta now thy grymme tole to the,
            And let se how thou cnokes."
            "Gladly, sir, for sothe,"
            Quoth Gawan; his ax he strokes.

The grene knyght upon grounde graythely hym dresses:
A littel lut with the hede, the lere he discoveres;
His longe lovelych lokkes he layd over his croun,
420 Let the naked nec to the note schewe.

390 "Gawain," said the green knight, "by God, I'm glad
the favor I've called for will fall from your fist.
You've perfectly repeated the promise we've made
and the terms of the contest are crystal clear.
Except for one thing: you must solemnly swear
that you'll seek me yourself; that you'll search me out
to the ends of the earth to earn the same blow
as you'll dole out today in this decorous hall."
"But where will you be? Where's your abode?
You're a man of mystery, as God is my maker.
400 Which court do you come from and what are you called?
There is knowledge I need, including your name,
then by wit I'll work out the way to your door
and keep to our contract, so cross my heart."
"But enough at New Year. It needs nothing more,"
said the war man in green to worthy Gawain.
"I could tell you the truth once you've taken the blow;
if you smite me smartly I could spell out the facts
of my house and home and my name, if it helps,
then you'll pay me a visit and vouch for our pact.
410 Or if I keep quiet you might cope much better,
loafing and lounging here, looking no further. But
                    you stall!
          Now grasp that gruesome axe
          and show your striking style."
          He answered, "Since you ask,"
          and touched the tempered steel.

In the standing position he prepared to be struck,
bent forward, revealing a flash of green flesh
as he heaped his hair to the crown of his head,
420 the nape of his neck now naked and ready.

Gauan gripped to his ax and gederes hit on hyght,
The kay fot on the folde he before sette,
Let hit doun lyghtly lyght on the naked,
That the scharp of the schalk schyndered the bones,
And schrank thurgh the schyire grece, and scade hit in twynne,
That the bit of the broun stel bot on the grounde.
The fayre hede fro the halce hit to the erthe,
That fele hit foyned wyth her fete, there hit forth roled;
The blod brayd fro the body, that blykked on the grene.
430 And nawther faltered ne fel the freke never the helder,
Bot stythly he start forth upon styf schonkes,
And runyschly he raght out, there as renkkes stoden,
Laght to his lufly hed, and lyft hit up sone;
And sythen bowes to his blonk, the brydel he cachches,
Steppes into stel-bawe and strydes alofte,
And his hede by the here in his honde haldes.
And as sadly the segge hym in his sadel sette
As non unhap had hym ayled, thagh hedles nowe
                    in stedde.
440 He brayde his bluk aboute,
                That ugly bodi that bledde;
                Moni on of hym had doute,
                Bi that his resouns were redde.

For the hede in his honde he haldes up even,
Toward the derrest on the dece he dresses the face;
And hit lyfte up the yye-lyddes, and loked ful brode,
And meled thus much with his muthe, as ye may now here:
"Loke, Gawan, thou be graythe to go as thou hettes,
And layte as lelly til thou me, lude, fynde,
450 As thou has hette in this halle, herande thise knyghtes.
To the grene chapel thou chose, I charge the, to fotte

Gawain grips the axe and heaves it heavenwards,
plants his left foot firmly on the floor in front,
then swings it swiftly towards the bare skin.
The cleanness of the strike cleaved the spinal cord
and parted the fat and the flesh so far
that the bright steel blade took a bite from the floor.
The handsome head tumbles onto the earth
and the king's men kick it as it clatters past.
Blood gutters brightly against his green gown,
430 yet the man doesn't shudder or stagger or sink
but trudges towards them on those tree-trunk legs
and rummages around, reaches at their feet
and cops hold of his head and hoists it high,
and strides to his steed, snatches the bridle,
steps into the stirrup and swings into the saddle
still gripping his head by a handful of hair.
Then he settles himself in his seat with the ease
of a man unmarked, never mind being minus
          his head!
440 And when he wheeled about
        his bloody neck still bled.
        His point was proved. The court
        was deadened now with dread.

For that scalp and skull now swung from his fist;
towards the top table he turned the face
and it opened its eyelids, stared straight ahead
and spoke this speech, which you'll hear for yourselves:
"Sir Gawain, be wise enough to keep your word
and faithfully follow me until I'm found
450 as you vowed in this hall within hearing of these horsemen.
You're charged with getting to the Green Chapel,

Such a dunt as thou has dalt—disserved thou habbes—

To be yederly yolden on Nw Yeres morn.

The knyght of the grene chapel men knowen me mony;

Forthi me for to fynde, if thou fraystes, fayles thou never.

Therfore com, other recreaunt be calde the behoveus."

With a runisch rout the raynes he tornes,

Halled out at the hal-dor, his hed in his hande,

That the fyr of the flynt flawe fro fole hoves.

460 To quat kyth he becom knwe non there,

Never more then thay wyste fram quethen he was wonnen.

What thenne?

The kyng and Gawen thare

At that grene thay laghe and grenne;

Yet breved was hit ful bare

A mervayl among tho menne.

Thagh Arther the hende kyng at hert hade wonder,

He let no semblaunt be sene, bot sayde ful hyghe

To the comlych quene, wyth cortays speche:

470 "Dere dame, to-day demay yow never;

Wel bycommes such craft upon Cristmasse,

Laykyng of enterludes, to laghe and to syng

Among thise kynde caroles of knyghtes and ladyes.

Never-the-lece to my mete I may me wel dres,

For I haf sen a selly, I may not forsake."

He glent upon Sir Gawen and gaynly he sayde:

"Now sir, heng up thyn ax, that has innogh hewen."

And hit was don abof the dece, on doser to henge,

Ther alle men for mervayl myght on hit loke,

480 And bi trwe tytel therof to telle the wonder.

Thenne thay bowed to a borde thise burnes togeder,

The kyng and the gode knyght, and kene men hem served

to reap what you've sown. You'll rightfully receive
the justice you are due just as January dawns.
Men know my name as the Green Chapel knight
and even a fool couldn't fail to find me.
So come, or be called a coward forever."
With a tug of the reins he twisted around
and, head still in hand, galloped out of the hall,
so the hooves brought fire from the flame in the flint.
460　Which kingdom he came from they hadn't a clue,
no more than they knew where he made for next.

And then?

Well, with the green man gone
they laughed and grinned again.
And yet such goings-on
were magic to those men.

And although King Arthur was awestruck at heart
no sign of it showed. Instead he spoke
to his queen of queens with courteous words:
470　"Dear lady, don't be daunted by this deed today,
it's in keeping that such strangeness should occur at Christmas
between sessions of banter and seasonal song,
amid the lively pastimes of ladies and lords.
And at least I'm allowed to eat at last,
having witnessed such wonder, wouldn't you say?"
Then he glanced at Gawain and was graceful with his words:
"Now hang up your axe—one hack is enough."
So it dangled from the drape behind the dais
so that men who saw it would be mesmerised and amazed,
480　and give voice, on its evidence, to that stunning event.
Then the two of them turned and walked to the table,
the monarch and his man, and were met with food—

Of alle dayntyes double, as derrest myght falle,
Wyth alle maner of mete and mynstralcie bothe.
Wyth wele walt thay that day, til worthed an ende
in londe.
Now thenk wel, Sir Gawan,
For wothe that thou ne wonde
This aventure for to frayn,
That thou has tan on honde.

490

double dishes apiece, rare delicacies,
all manner of meals—and the music of minstrels.
And they danced and sang till the sun went down
                    that day.
            But mind your mood, Gawain,
            keep blacker thoughts at bay,
            or loose this lethal game
490   you've promised you will play.

This hanselle has Arthur of aventurus on fyrst
In yonge yer, for he yerned yelpyng to here.
Thagh hym wordes were wane when thay to sete wenten,
Now ar thay stoken of sturne werk, stafful her hond.
Gawan was glad to begynne those gomnes in halle,
Bot thagh the ende be hevy, haf ye no wonder;
For thagh men ben mery in mynde quen thay han mayn drynk,
A yere yernes ful yerne, and yeldes never lyke;
The forme to the fynisment foldes ful selden.
500 Forthi this Yol overyede, and the yere after,
And uche sesoun serlepes sued after other;
After Crystenmasse com the crabbed Lentoun,
That fraystes flesch wyth the fysche and fode more symple.
Bot thenne the weder of the worlde wyth wynter hit threpes,
Colde clenges adoun, cloudes uplyften,
Schyre schedes the rayn in schowres ful warme,
Falles upon fayre flat, flowres there schewen.
Bothe groundes and the greves grene ar her wedes,
Bryddes busken to bylde, and bremlych syngen
510 For solace of the softe somer that sues therafter
                    bi bonk;
              And blossumes bolne to blowe
              Bi rawes rych and ronk,

FITT II

This happening was a gift—just as Arthur had asked for
and had yearned to hear of while the year was young.
And if guests had no subject as they strolled to their seats,
now they chattered of Gawain's chances in this challenge.
And Gawain had been glad to begin the game,
but don't be so shocked should the plot turn pear-shaped:
for men might be merry when addled with mead
but each year, short lived, is unlike the last
and rarely resolves in the style it arrived.
So the festival finishes and a new year follows
in eternal sequence, season by season.
After lavish Christmas come the lean days of Lent
when the flesh is tested with fish and simple food.
Then the world's weather wages war on winter:
cold shrinks earthwards and the clouds climb;
sun-warmed, shimmering rain comes showering
onto meadows and fields where flowers unfurl;
woods and grounds wear a wardrobe of green;
birds burble with life and build busily
as summer spreads, settling on slopes as
                    it should.
            Now every hedgerow brims
            with blossom and with bud,

Then notes noble innoghe
Ar herde in wod so wlonk.

After, the sesoun of somer wyth the soft wyndes,
Quen Zeferus syfles hymself on sedes and erbes;
Wela wynne is the wort that waxes theroute,
When the donkande dewe dropes of the leves,
520 To bide a blysful blusch of the bryght sunne.
Bot then hyyes hervest, and hardenes hym sone,
Warnes hym for the wynter to wax ful rype;
He dryves wyth droght the dust for to ryse,
Fro the face of the folde to flyye ful hyghe;
Wrothe wynde of the welkyn wrasteles with the sunne,
The leves laucen fro the lynde and lyghten on the grounde,
And al grayes the gres that grene was ere;
Thenne al rypes and rotes that ros upon fyrst.
And thus yirnes the yere in yisterdayes mony,
530 And wynter wyndes ayayn, as the worlde askes,
          no fage,
          Til Meghelmas mone
          Was cumen wyth wynter wage.
          Then thenkkes Gawan ful sone
          Of his anious vyage.

Yet quyl Al-hal-day with Arther he lenges,
And he made a fare on that fest, for the frekes sake,
With much revel and ryche of the Rounde Table.
Knyghtes ful cortays and comlych ladies,
540 Al for luf of that lede in longynge thay were;
Bot never-the-lece ne the later thay nevened bot merthe,
Mony joyles for that jentyle japes ther maden.
For aftter mete with mournyng he meles to his eme,

and lively songbirds sing
from lovely, leafy woods.

So summer comes in season with its subtle airs,
when the west wind sighs among shoots and seeds,
and those plants which flower and flourish are a pleasure
as their leaves let drip their drink of dew
520   and they sparkle and glitter when glanced by sunlight.
Then autumn arrives to harden the harvest
and with it comes a warning to ripen before winter.
The drying airs arrive, driving up dust
from the face of the earth to the heights of heaven,
and wild sky wrestles the sun with its winds,
and the leaves of the lime lay littered on the ground,
and grass that was green turns withered and gray.
Then all which had risen over-ripens and rots
and yesterday on yesterday the year dies away,
530   and winter returns, as is the way of the world
                         through time.
                 At Michaelmas the moon
                 stands like that season's sign,
                 a warning to Gawain
                 to rouse himself and ride.

Yet by All Saints' Day he was still at Arthur's side,
and they feasted in the name of their noble knight
with the revels and riches of the Round Table.
The lords of that hall and their loving ladies
540   were sad and concerned for the sake of their knight,
but nevertheless they made light of his load.
Those joyless at his plight made jokes and rejoiced.
Then sorrowfully, after supper, he spoke with his uncle,

And spekes of his passage, and pertly he sayde:

"Now, lege lorde of my lyf, leve I yow ask.

Ye knowe the cost of this cace, kepe I no more

To telle yow tenes therof, never bot trifel;

Bot I am boun to the bur barely to-morne,

To sech the gome of the grene, as God wyl me wysse."

550 Thenne the best of the burgh bowed togeder,

Aywan and Errik and other ful mony,

Sir Doddinaval de Savage, the duk of Clarence,

Launcelot and Lyonel and Lucan the gode,

Sir Boos and Sir Bydver, big men bothe,

And mony other menskful, with Mador de la Port.

Alle this compayny of court com the kyng nerre,

For to counseyl the knyght, with care at her hert.

There was much derne doel driven in the sale,

That so worthé as Wawan schulde wende on that ernde,

560 To dryye a delful dynt, and dele no more

wyth bronde.

The knyght mad ay god chere,

And sayde: "Quat schuld I wonde?

Of destinés derf and dere

What may mon do bot fonde?"

He dowelles ther al that day, and dresses on the morn,

Askes erly hys armes, and alle were thay broght.

Fyrst a tulé tapit, tyght over the flet,

And miche was the gyld gere that glent ther alofte.

570 The stif mon steppes theron, and the stel hondeles,

Dubbed in a dublet of a dere tars,

And sythen a crafty capados, closed aloft,

That wyth a bryght blaunner was bounden withinne.

Thenne set thay the sabatouns upon the segge fotes,

and openly talked of the trip he must take:

"Now, lord of my life, I must ask for your leave.

You were witness to my wager. I have no wish

to retell you the terms—they're nothing but a trifle.

I must set out tomorrow to receive that stroke

from the knight in green, and let God be my guide."

550   Then the cream of Camelot crowded around:

Ywain and Eric and others of that ilk,

Sir Dodinal the Dreaded, the Duke of Clarence,

Lancelot, Lionel, Lucan the Good,

and Sir Bors and Sir Bedevere—both big names,

and powerful men such as Mador de la Port.

This courtly committee approaches the king

to offer up heartfelt advice to our hero.

And sounds of sadness and sorrow were heard

that one as worthy and well liked as Gawain

560   should suffer that strike but offer no stroke in

reply.

Yet keeping calm the knight

just quipped, "Why should I shy

away. If fate is kind

or cruel, man still must try."

He remained all that day and in the morning he dressed,

asked early for his arms and all were produced.

First a rug of rare cloth was unrolled on the floor,

heaped with gear which glimmered and gleamed,

570   and onto it he stepped to receive his armored suit.

He tries on his tunic of extravagant silk,

then the neatly cut cloak, closed at the neck,

its lining finished with a layer of white fur.

Then they settled his feet into steel shoes

His leges lapped in stel with luflych greves,
With polaynes piched therto, policed ful clene,
Aboute his knes knaged wyth knotes of golde;
Queme quyssewes then, that coyntlych closed
His thik thrawen thyghes, with thwonges to tachched;
580 And sythen the brawden bryné of bryght stel rynges
Vmbeweved that wyy, upon wlonk stuffe;
And wel bornyst brace upon his bothe armes,
With gode cowters and gay, and gloves of plate,
And alle the godlych gere that hym gayn schulde
                    that tyde;
          Wyth ryche cote-armure,
          His gold spores spend with pryde,
          Gurde wyth a bront ful sure
          With silk sayn umbe his syde.

590 When he was hasped in armes, his harnays was ryche;
The lest lachet other loupe lemed of golde.
So harnayst as he was he herknes his masse,
Offred and honoured at the heghe auter.
Sythen he comes to the kyng and to his cort-feres,
Laches lufly his leve at lordes and ladyes;
And thay hym kyst and conveyed, bikende hym to Kryst.
Bi that was Gryngolet grayth, and gurde with a sadel
That glemed ful gayly with mony golde frenges,
Ayquere naylet ful nwe, for that note ryched;
600 The brydel barred aboute, with bryght golde bounden;
The apparayl of the payttrure and of the proude skyrtes,
The cropore and the covertor, acorded wyth the arsounes;
And al was rayled on red ryche golde nayles,
That al glytered and glent as glem of the sunne.
Thenne hentes he the helme, and hastily hit kysses,

and clad his calves, clamped them with greaves,
then hinged and highly polished plates
were knotted with gold thread to the knight's knees.
Then leg guards were fitted, lagging the flesh,
attached with thongs to his thick-set thighs.
580 Then comes the suit of shimmering steel rings
encasing his body and his costly clothes:
well burnished braces to both of his arms,
good elbow guards and glinting metal gloves,
all the trimmings and trappings of a knight tricked out
   to ride:
    a metal suit that shone;
    gold spurs which gleam with pride;
    a keen sword swinging from
    the silk belt to his side.

590 Fastened in his armor he seemed fabulous, famous,
every link looking golden to the very last loop.
Yet for all that metal he still made it to mass,
honored the Almighty before the high altar.
After which he comes to the king and his consorts
and asks to take leave of the ladies and lords;
they escort and kiss him and commended him to Christ.
Now Gringolet is rigged out and ready to ride
with a saddle which flickered with fine gold fringes
and was set with new studs for the special occasion.
600 The bridle was bound with stripes of bright gold,
the apparel of the panels was matched in appearance
to the color of the saddlebows and cropper and cover,
and nails of red gold were arrayed all around,
shining splendidly like splintered sunlight.
Then he holds up his helmet and kisses it without haste;

That was stapled stifly, and stoffed wythinne.

Hit was hyghe on his hede, hasped bihynde,

Wyth a lyghtly urysoun over the aventayle,

Enbrawden and bounden wyth the best gemmes

610 On brode sylkyn borde, and bryddes on semes,

As papjayes paynted pernyng bitwene,

Tortors and trulofes entayled so thyk

As mony burde theraboute had ben seven winter

in toune.

The cercle was more o prys

That umbeclypped hys croun,

Of diamauntes a devys

That bothe were bryght and broun.

Then thay schewed hym the schelde, that was of schyr goules,

620 Wyth the pentangel depaynt of pure golde hwes.

He braydes hit by the bauderyk, aboute the hals kestes,

That bisemed the segge semlyly fayre.

And quy the pentangel apendes to that prynce noble

I am intent yow to telle, thof tary hyt me schulde.

Hit is a syngne that Salamon set sumquyle

In bytoknyng of trawthe, bi tytle that hit habbes,

For hit is a figure that haldes fyve poyntes,

And uche lyne umbelappes and loukes in other,

And ayquere hit is endeles, and Englych hit callen

630 Overal, as I here, the endeles knot.

Forthy hit acordes to this knyght and to his cler armes,

For ay faythful in fyve and sere fyve sythes,

Gawan was for gode knawen and, as golde pured,

Voyded of uche vylany, wyth vertues ennourned

in mote.

Forthy the pentangel nwe

it was strongly stapled and its lining was stuffed,
and sat high on his head, fastened behind
with a colorful cloth to cover his neck
embroidered and bejeweled with brilliant gems
610   on the broad silk border, and with birds on the seams
such as painted parrots perched among periwinkles
and turtle doves and true lover's knots, tightly entwined
as if women had worked at it seven winters
        at least.
      The diamond diadem
      was greater still. It gleamed
      with flawless, flashing gems
      both clear and smoked, it seemed.

Then they showed him the shining scarlet shield
620   with its pentangle painted in pure gold.
He seized it by its strap and slung it round his neck;
he looked well in what he wore, and was worthy of it.
And why the pentangle was appropriate to that prince
I intend to say, though it will stall our story.
It is a symbol that Solomon once set in place
and is taken to this day as a token of fidelity,
for the form of the figure is a five-pointed star
and each line overlaps and links with the last
so is ever eternal, and when spoken of in England
630   is known by the name of the endless knot.
So it suits this soldier in his spotless armor,
fully faithful in five ways five times over.
For Gawain was as good as the purest gold—
devoid of vices but virtuous, loyal
        and kind,
      so bore that badge on both

He ber in schelde and cote,
As tulk of tale most trwe
And gentylest knyght of lote.

640 Fyrst he was funden fautles in his fyve wyttes,
And efte fayled never the freke in his fyve fyngres,
And alle his afyaunce upon folde was in the fyve woundes
That Cryst kaght on the croys, as the crede telles.
And quere-so-ever thys mon in melly was stad,
His thro thoght was in that, thurgh alle other thynges,
That alle his forsnes he fong at the fyve joyes
That the hende heven quene had of hir chylde;
At this cause the knyght comlyche hade
In the inore half of his schelde hir ymage depaynted,
650 That quen he blusched therto his belde never payred.
The fyft fyve that I finde that the frek used
Was fraunchyse and felawschyp forbe al thyng;
His clannes and his cortaysye croked were never,
And pité, that passes alle poyntes—thyse pure fyve
Were harder happed on that hathel then on any other.
Now alle these fyve sythes, for sothe, were fetled on this knyght,
And uchone halched in other, that non ende hade,
And fyched upon fyve poyntes that fayld never,
Ne samned never in no syde, ne sundred nouther,
660 Withouten ende at any noke noquere, I fynde,
Where-ever the gomen bygan or glod to an ende.
Therfore on his schene schelde schapen was the knot
Ryally wyth red golde upon rede gowles,
That is the pure pentaungel wyth the peple called
with lore.
Now graythed is Gawan gay,
And laght his launce ryght thore,

his shawl and shield alike.
A prince who talked the truth.
A notable. A knight.

640 First he was deemed flawless in his five senses;
and secondly his five fingers were never at fault;
and thirdly his faith was founded in the five wounds
Christ received on the cross, as the creed recalls.
And fourthly, if that soldier struggled in skirmish
one thought pulled him through above all other things:
the fortitude he found in the five joys
which Mary had conceived in her son, our Savior.
For precisely that reason the princely rider
had the shape of her image inside his shield,
650 so by catching her eye his courage would not crack.
The fifth set of five which I heard the knight followed
included friendship and fraternity with fellow men,
purity and politeness that impressed at all times,
and pity, which surpassed all pointedness. Five things
which meant more to Gawain than to most other men.
So these five sets of five were fixed in this knight,
each linked to the last through the endless line,
a five-pointed form which never failed,
never stronger to one side or slack at the other,
660 but unbroken in its being from beginning to end
however its trail is tracked and traced.
So the star on the spangling shield he sported
shone royally, in gold, on a ruby red background,
the pure pentangle as people have called it
                for years.
        Then, lance in hand, held high,
        and got up in his gear

And gef hem alle goud day—
He wende for ever more.

670 He sperred the sted with the spures, and sprong on his way
So stif that the ston-fyr stroke out therafter.
Al that sey that semly syked in hert,
And sayde sothly al same segges til other,
Carande for that comly: "Bi Kryst, hit is scathe
That thou, leude, schal be lost, that art of lyf noble!
To fynde hys fere upon folde, in fayth, is not ethe.
Warloker to haf wroght had more wyt bene,
And haf dyght yonder dere a duk to have worthed.
A lowande leder of ledes in londe hym wel semes,
680 And so had better haf ben then britned to noght,
Hadet wyth an alvisch mon, for angardes pryde.
Who knew ever any kyng such counsel to take
As knyghtes in cavelaciouns on Crystmasse gomnes?"
Wel much was the warme water that waltered of yyen,
When that semly syre soght fro tho wones
                    thad daye.
              He made non abode,
              Bot wyghtly went hys way;
              Mony wylsum way he rode,
690   The bok as I herde say.

Now rides this renk thurgh the ryalme of Logres,
Sir Gauan, on Godes halve, thagh hym no gomen thoght.
Oft leudles alone he lenges on nyghtes,
Ther he fonde noght hym byfore the fare that he lyked.
Hade he no fere bot his fole bi frythes and dounes,
Ne no gome bot God bi gate wyth to karp,
Til that he neghed ful neghe into the Northe Wales.

he bids them all good-bye
one final time, he fears.

670   Spiked with the spurs the steed sped away
with such force that the fire-stones sparked underfoot.
All sighed at the sight, and with sinking hearts
they whispered their worries to one another,
concerned for their comrade. "A pity, by Christ,
if a lord so noble should lose his life.
To find his equal on earth would be far from easy.
Cleverer to have acted with caution and care,
deemed him a duke—a title he was due—
a leader of men, lord of many lands;
680   better that than being battered into oblivion,
beheaded by an ogre through headstrong pride.
How unknown for a king to take counsel of a knight
in the grip of an engrossing Christmas game."
Warm tears welled up in their weepy eyes
as gallant Sir Gawain galloped from court
that day.
He sped from home and hearth
and went his winding way
on steep and snaking paths,
690   just as the story says.

Now through England's realm he rides and rides,
Sir Gawain, God's servant, on his grim quest,
passing long dark nights unloved and alone,
foraging to feed, finding little to call food,
with no friend but his horse through forests and hills
and only our Lord in heaven to hear him.
He wanders near to the north of Wales

Alle the iles of Anglesay on lyft half he haldes,
And fares over the fordes by the forlondes,
700 Over at the Holy Hede, til he hade eft bonk
In the wyldrenesse of Wyrale—wonde ther bot lyte
That auther God other gome wyth goud hert lovied.
And ay he frayned, as he ferde, at frekes that he met,
If thay hade herde any karp of a knyght grene,
In any grounde theraboute, of the grene chapel;
And al nykked hym wyth nay, that never in her lyve
Thay seye never no segge that was of suche hews
        of grene.
    The knyght tok gates straunge
710   In mony a bonk unbene;
    His cher ful oft con chaunge,
    That chapel er he myght sene.

Mony klyf he overclambe in contrayes straunge,
Fer floten fro his frendes fremedly he rydes.
At uche warthe other water ther the wyye passed
He fonde a foo hym byfore, bot ferly hit were,
And that so foule and so felle that feght hym byhode.
So mony mervayl bi mount ther the mon fyndes,
Hit were to tore for to telle of the tenthe dole.
720 Sumwhyle wyth wormes he werres, and with wolves als,
Sumwhyle wyth wodwos that woned in the knarres,
Bothe wyth bulles and beres, and bores otherquyle,
And etaynes that hym anelede of the heghe felle.
Nade he ben dughty and dryye, and dryghtyn had served,
Douteles he hade ben ded and dreped ful ofte,
For werre wrathed hym not so much, that wynter was wors,
When the colde cler water fro the cloudes schadde,
And fres er hit falle myght to the fale erthe.

with the Isles of Anglesey off to the left.
He keeps to the coast, fording each course,
crossing at Holy Head and coming ashore
in the wilds of the Wirral, whose wayward people
both God and good men have quite given up on.
And he constantly enquires of those he encounters
if they know, or not, in this neck of the woods,
of a great green man or a Green Chapel.
No, they say, never. Never in their lives.
They know of neither a chap nor a chapel
           so strange.
       He trails through bleak terrain.
       His mood and manner change
       at every twist and turn
       towards that chosen church.

In a strange region he scales steep slopes;
far from his friends he cuts a lonely figure.
Where he bridges a brook or wades through a waterway
ill fortune brings him face-to-face with a foe
so foul or fierce he is bound to use force.
So momentous are his travels among the mountains
to tell just a tenth would be a tall order.
Here he scraps with serpents and snarling wolves,
here he tangles with wodwos causing trouble in the crags,
or with bulls and bears and the odd wild boar.
Hard on his heels through the highlands come giants.
Only diligence and faith in the face of death
will keep him from becoming a corpse or carrion.
And the wars were one thing, but winter was worse:
clouds shed their cargo of crystallized rain
which froze as it fell to the frost-glazed earth.

Ner slayn wyth the slete he sleped in his yrnes
730   Mo nyghtes then innoghe in naked rokkes,
Ther as claterande fro the crest the colde borne rennes,
And henged heghe over his hede in hard ysse-ikkles.
Thus in peryl and payne and plytes ful harde
Bi contray caryes this knyght tyl Krystmasse even,
        al one.
        The knyght wel that tyde
        To Mary made his mone,
        That ho hym red to ryde,
        And wysse hym to sum wone.

740   Bi a mounte on the morne meryly he rydes
Into a forest ful dep, that ferly was wylde,
Highe hilles on uche a halve, and holtwodes under
Of hore okes ful hoge a hundreth togeder.
The hasel and the hawthorne were harled al samen,
With roghe raged mosse rayled aywhere,
With mony bryddes unblythe upon bare twyges,
That pitosly ther piped for pyne of the colde.
The gome upon Gryngolet glydes hem under
Thurgh mony misy and myre, mon al hym one,
750   Carande for his costes, lest he ne kever schulde
To se the servyse of that syre, that on that self nyght
Of a burde was borne, oure baret to quelle.
And therfore sykyng he sayde: "I beseche the, Lorde,
And Mary, that is myldest moder so dere,
Of sum herber ther heghly I myght here masse
Ande thy matynes to-morne, mekely I ask,
And therto prestly I pray my pater and ave
        and crede."
        He rode in his prayere,

With nerves frozen numb he napped in his armor,
730 bivouacked in the blackness amongst bare rocks
where meltwater streamed from the snow-capped summits
and high overhead hung chandeliers of ice.
So in peril and pain Sir Gawain made progress,
crisscrossing the countryside until Christmas
                    Eve. Then
            at that time of tiding,
            he prayed to highest heaven.
            Let Mother Mary guide him
            towards some house or haven.

740 Next morning he moves on, skirts the mountainside,
descends a deep forest, densely overgrown,
with ancient oaks in huddles of hundreds
and vaulting hills above each half of the valley.
Hazel and hawthorn are interwoven,
decked and draped in damp, shaggy moss,
and bedraggled birds on bare, black branches
pipe pitifully into the piercing cold.
Under cover of the canopy he girded Gringolet
through mud and marshland, a most mournful man,
750 concerned and afraid in case he should fail
in the worship of our Deity, who, on that date
was born the Virgin's son to save our souls.
He prayed with heavy heart. "Father, hear me,
and Lady Mary, our mother most mild,
let me happen on some house where mass might be heard,
and matins in the morning; meekly I ask,
and here I utter my pater, ave
                    and creed."
            He rides the path and prays,

760 　　　　And cryed for his mysdede;
　　　　　　He sayned hym in sythes sere
　　　　　　And sayde: "Cros Kryst me spede!"

Nade he sayned hymself, segge, bot thrye,
Er he was war in the wod of a won in a mote,
Abof a launde, on a lawe, loken under boghes
Of mony borelych bole aboute bi the diches:
A castel the comlokest that ever knyght aghte,
Pyched on a prayere, a park al aboute,
With a pyked palays, pyned ful thik,
770 That umbeteye mony tre mo then two myle.
That holde on that on syde the hathel avysed,
As hit schemered and schon thurgh the schyre okes.
Thenne has he hendly of his helme, and heghly he thonkes
Jesus and sayn Gilyan, that gentyle ar bothe,
That cortaysly hade hym kydde and his cry herkened.
"Now bone hostel," cothe the burne, "I beseche yow yette!"
Thenne gerdes he to Gryngolet with the gilt heles,
And he ful chauncely has chosen to the chef gate,
That broght bremly the burne to the bryge ende
780 　　　　　　　in haste.
　　　　　　The bryge was breme upbrayde,
　　　　　　The yates wer stoken faste,
　　　　　　The walles were wel arayed—
　　　　　　Hit dut no wyndes blaste.

The burne bode on bonk, that on blonk hoved,
Of the depe double dich that drof to the place.
The walle wod in the water wonderly depe,
Ande eft a ful huge heght hit haled upon lofte,
Of harde hewen ston up to the tables,

760   dismayed by his misdeeds,

and signs Christ's cross and says,

"Be near me in my need."

No sooner had he signed himself three times

than he became aware, in those woods, of high walls

in a moat, on a mound, bordered by the boughs

of thick-trunked timber which trimmed the water.

The most commanding castle a knight ever kept,

positioned in a site of sweeping parkland

with a palisade of pikes pitched in the earth

770 in the midst of tall trees for two miles or more.

From the corner of his eye this castle became clearer

as it sparkled and shone within shimmering oaks,

and with helmet in hand he offered up thanks

to Jesus and Saint Julian, both gentle and good,

who had courteously heard him and heeded his cry.

"A lodging at last. So allow it, my Lord."

Then he girded Gringolet with his gilded spurs,

and purely by chance chose the principal approach

to the building, which brought him to the end of the bridge

780   with haste.

The drawbridge stood withdrawn,

the front gates were shut fast.

Such well-constructed walls

would blunt the storm wind's blast.

In the saddle of his steed he halts on the slope

of the delving moat with its double ditch.

Out of water of wondrous depth, the walls

then loomed overhead to a heavenly height,

course after course of crafted stone,

790 Enbaned under the abataylment in the best lawe;

And sythen garytes ful gaye gered bitwene,

Wyth mony luflych loupe that louked ful clene:

A better barbican that burne bluched upon never.

And innermore he behelde that halle ful hyghe,

Towres telded bytwene, trochet ful thik,

Fayre fylyoles that fyyed, and ferlyly long,

With corvon coprounes craftyly sleye.

Chalkwhyt chymnees ther ches he innoghe,

Upon bastel roves that blenked ful quyte.

800 So mony pynakle payntet was poudred ayquere

Among the castel carneles, clambred so thik,

That pared out of papure purely hit semed.

The fre freke on the fole hit fayre innoghe thoght,

If he myght kever to com the cloyster wythinne,

To herber in that hostel whyl halyday lested,

avinant.

He calde, and sone ther com

A porter pure plesaunt.

On the wal his ernd he nome,

810 And haylsed the knyght erraunt.

"Gode sir," quoth Gawan, "woldes thou go myn ernde

To the hegh lorde of this hous, herber to crave?"

"Ye, Peter," quoth the porter, "and purely I trowee

That ye be, wyye, welcum to won quyle yow lykes."

Then yede the wyye ayayn swythe,

And folke frely hym wyth, to fonge the knyght.

Thay let doun the grete draght and derely out yeden,

And kneled doun on her knes upon the colde erthe

To welcum this ilk wyy, as worthy hom thoght.

820 Thay yolden hym the brode yate, yarked up wyde,

then battlements embellished in the boldest style

and turrets arranged around the ramparts

with lockable loopholes set into the lookouts.

The knight had not seen a more stunning structure.

Further in, his eye was drawn to a hall

attended, architecturally, by many tall towers

with a series of spires spiking the air

all crowned by carvings exquisitely cut.

Uncountable chimneys the color of chalk

sprutted from the roof and sparkled in the sun.

So perfect was that vision of painted pinnacles

clustered within the castle's enclosure

it appeared that the place was cut from paper.

Then a notion occurred to that noble knight:

to inveigle a visit, get invited inside,

to be hosted and housed, and all the holy days

             remain.

        Responding to his call

        a pleasant porter came,

        a watchman on the wall,

        who welcomed Sir Gawain.

"Good morning," said our man, "will you bear a message

to the owner of this hall and ask him for shelter?"

"By Saint Peter," said the porter, "it'll be my pleasure,

and I'm willing to bet you'll be welcome to a bed."

Then he went on his way, but came back at once

with a group who had gathered to greet the stranger;

the drawbridge came down and they crossed the ditch

and knelt in the frost in front of the knight

to welcome this man in a way deemed worthy.

Then they yielded to their guest, yanked open the gate,

And he hem raysed rekenly and rod over the brygge.

Sere segges hym sesed by sadel, quel he lyght,

And sythen stabeled his stede stif men innoghe.

Knyghtes and swyeres comen doun thenne

For to bryng this buurne wyth blys into halle.

Quen he hef up his helme, ther hiyed innoghe

For to hent hit at his honde, the hende to serven;

His bronde and his blasoun bothe thay token.

Then haylsed he ful hendly tho hatheles uchone,

830 And mony proud mon ther presed, that prynce to honour.

Alle hasped in his hegh wede to halle thay hym wonnen,

Ther fayre fyre upon flet fersly brenned.

Thenne the lorde of the lede loutes fro his chambre

For to mete wyth menske the mon on the flor.

He sayde: "Ye ar welcum to wone as yow lykes.

That here is, al is yowre awen, to have at yowre wylle

      and welde."

    "Graunt mercy," quoth Gawayn,

    "Ther Kryst hit yow foryelde."

840   As frekes that semed fayn

    Ayther other in armes con felde.

Gawayn glyght on the gome that godly hym gret,

And thught hit a bolde burne that the burgh aghte,

A hoge hathel for the nones, and of hyghe eldee;

Brode, bryght was his berde, and al bever-hwed,

Sturne, stif on the stryththe on stalworth schonkes,

Felle face as the fyre, and fre of hys speche;

And wel hym semed for sothe, as the segge thught,

To lede a lortschyp in lee of leudes ful gode.

850 The lorde hym charred to a chambre, and chefly cumaundes

To delyver hym a leude, hym lowly to serve;

and bidding them to rise he rode across the bridge.
He was assisted from the saddle by several men
and the strongest amongst them stabled his steed.
Then knights, and the squires of knights, drew near,
to escort him, with courtesy, into the castle.
As he took off his helmet, many hasty hands
reached out to receive it and to serve this stranger,
and his sword and his shield were taken aside.
Then he made himself known to nobles and knights
830 and proud fellows pressed forwards to confer their respects.
Still heavy with armor he was led to the hall
where a fire burned bright with the fiercest flames.
Then the master of the manor emerged from his chamber,
to greet him in the hall with all due honor,
saying, "Behave in my house as your heart pleases.
To whatever you want you are welcome, do what
              you will."
           "My thanks," Gawain exclaimed,
           "May Christ reward you well."
840   Then firmly, like good friends,
              they hugged and held awhile.

Gawain gazed at the lord who greeted him so gracefully,
the great one who governed that grand estate,
powerful and large, in the prime of his life,
with a bushy beard as red as a beaver's,
steady in his stance, solid of build,
with a fiery face but with fine conversation:
a man quite capable, it occurred to Gawain,
of keeping such a castle and captaining his knights.
850 Escorted to his quarters the lord quickly orders
that a servant be assigned to assist Gawain,

And there were boun at his bode burnes innoghe
That broght hym to a bryght boure, ther beddying was noble
Of cortynes of clene sylk wyth cler golde hemmes,
And covertores ful curious with comlych panes,
Of bryght blaunmer above enbrawded bisydes,
Rudeles rennande on ropes, red golde rynges,
Tapytes tyght to the wowe, of Tuly and Tars,
And under fete, on the flet, of folwande sute.
860 Ther he was dispoyled, wyth speches of myerthe,
The burn of his bruny and of his bryght wedes.
Ryche robes ful rad renkkes hym broghten,
For to charge and to chaunge and chose of the best.
Sone as he on hent, and happed therinne,
That sete on hym semly, wyth saylande skyrtes,
The ver by his visage verayly hit semed
Welnegh to uche hathel, alle on hwes,
Lowande and lufly, alle his lymmes under,
That a comloker knyght never Kryst made,
870   hem thoght.
               Whethen in worlde he were,
               Hit semed as he moght
               Be prynce withouten pere
               In felde ther felle men foght.

A cheyer byfore the chemné, ther charcole brenned,
Was graythed for Sir Gawan graythely with clothes,
Whyssynes upon queldepoyntes that koynt wer bothe.
And thenne a mere mantyle was on that mon cast
Of a broun bleeaunt, enbrauded ful ryche,
880 And fayre furred wythinne with felles of the best—
Alle of ermyn in erde—his hode of the same.
And he sete in that settel semlych ryche,

and many were willing to wait on his word.
They brought him to a bedroom, beautifully furnished
with fine silken fabrics finished in gold
and curious coverlets lavishly quilted
in bloodless ermine and embroidered to each border.
Curtains ran on cords through red-gold rings,
tapestries from Toulouse and Turkistan
were fixed against walls and fitted underfoot.
860   With humorous banter Gawain was helped out
of his chain-mail coat and costly clothes,
then they rushed to bring him an array of robes
of the choicest cloth. He chose, and changed,
and as soon as he stood in that stunning gown
with its flowing skirts which suited his shape
it almost appeared to the persons present
that spring, with its spectrum of colors, had sprung;
so alive and lean were that young man's limbs
a nobler creature Christ had never created, they declared.
870   This knight,
           whose country was unclear,
           now seemed to them by sight
           a prince without a peer
           in fields where fierce men fight.

In front of a flaming fireside a chair
was pulled into place for Gawain, and padded
with covers and quilts all cleverly stitched,
then a cape was cast across the knight
of rich brown cloth with embroidered borders,
880   finished inside with the finest furs,
ermine, to be exact, and a hood which echoed it.
Resplendently dressed he settled in his seat;

And achaufed hym chefly, and thenne his cher mended.

Sone was telded up a tabil on trestes ful fayre,

Clad wyth a clene clothe that cler quyt schewed,

Sanap and salure and sylverin spones.

The wyye wesche at his wylle, and went to his mete.

Segges hym served semly innoghe

Wyth sere sewes and sete, sesounde of the best,

890 Double-felde, as hit falles, and fele kyn fisches,

Summe baken in bred, summe brad on the gledes,

Summe sothen, summe in sewe savered with spyces,

And ay sawses so sleye that the segge lyked.

The freke calde hit a fest ful frely and ofte

Ful hendely, quen alle the hatheles rehayted hym at ones

     as hende:

    "This penaunce now ye take,

    And eft hit schal amende."

    That mon much merthe con make,

900   For wyn in his hed that wende.

Thenne was spyed and spured upon spare wyse

Bi prevé poyntes of that prynce, put to hymselven,

That he beknew cortaysly of the court that he were,

That athel Arthure the hende haldes hym one,

That is the ryche ryal kyng of the Rounde Table;

And hit was Wawen hymself that in that won syttes,

Comen to that Krystmasse, as case hym then lymped.

When the lorde hade lerned that he the leude hade,

Loude laghed he therat, so lef hit hym thoght,

910 And alle the men in that mote maden much joye

To apere in his presense prestly that tyme,

That alle prys and prowes and pured thewes

Apendes to hys persoun, and praysed is ever;

as his limbs thawed, so his thoughts lightened.
Soon a table was set on sturdy trestles
covered entirely with a clean white cloth
and cruets of salt and silver spoons.
In a while he washed and went to his meal.
Staff came quickly and served him in style
with several soups all seasoned to taste,
890 double helpings as was fitting, and a feast of fish,
some baked in bread, some browned over flames,
some boiled or steamed, some stewed in spices
and subtle sauces to tantalize his tongue.
Four or five times he called it a feast,
and the courteous company happily cheered him
　　　　　along:
　　　　"On penance plates you dine—
　　　　there's better board to come."
　　　　The warming, heady wine
900 　　　then freed his mind for fun.

Now through tactful talk and tentative enquiry
polite questions are put to this prince;
he responds respectfully, and speaks of his journey
from the Court of Arthur, King of Camelot,
royalty, and ruler of the Round Table,
and he says they now sit with Gawain himself,
who has come here at Christmastime quite by chance.
Once the master has gathered that his guest is Gawain
he thinks it so thrilling he laughs out loud.
910 All the men of that manor were of the same mind,
being keen and quick to appear in his presence,
this person famed for prowess and purity,
whose noble skills were sung to the skies,

Byfore alle men upon molde his mensk is the most.

Uch segge ful softly sayde to his fere:

"Now schal we semlych se sleghtes of thewes

And the teccheles termes of talkyng noble.

Wich spede is in speche, unspurd may we lerne,

Syn we haf fonged that fyne fader of nurture.

920 God has geven uus his grace godly for sothe,

That such a gest as Gawan grauntes uus to have,

When burnes blythe of his burthe schal sitte

            and synge.

        In menyng of maneres mere

        This burne now schal uus bryng.

        I hope that may hym here

        Schal lerne of luf-talkyng."

Bi that the diner was done and the dere up,

Hit was negh at the niyght neghed the tyme.

930 Chaplaynes to the chapeles chosen the gate,

Rungen ful rychely, ryght as thay schulden,

To the hersum evensong of the hyghe tyde.

The lorde loutes therto, and the lady als;

Into a cumly closet coyntly ho entres.

Gawan glydes ful gay and gos theder sone;

The lorde laches hym by the lappe and ledes hym to sytte,

And couthly hym knowes and calles hym his nome,

And sayde he was the welcomest wyye of the worlde;

And he hym thonkked throly, and ayther halched other,

940 And seten soberly samen the servise-quyle.

Thenne lyst the lady to loke on the knyght;

Thenne com ho of hir closet with mony cler burdes.

Ho was the fayrest in felle, of flesche and of lyre,

And of compas and colour and costes, of alle other,

whose life was the stuff of legend and lore.
Then knight spoke softly to knight, saying
"Watch now, we'll witness his graceful ways,
hear the faultless phrasing of flawless speech;
if we listen we will learn the merits of language
since we have in our hall a man of high honor.

920 Ours is a generous and giving God
to grant that we welcome Gawain as our guest
as we sing of His birth who was born to save us.
        We few
            shall learn a lesson here
            in tact and manners true,
            and hopefully we'll hear
            love's tender language, too."

Once dinner was done Gawain drew to his feet
and darkness neared as day became dusk.
930 Chaplains went off to the castle's chapels
to sound the bells hard, to signal the hour
of evensong, summoning each and every soul.
The lord goes alone, then his lady arrives,
concealing herself in a private pew.
Gawain attends, too; tugged by his sleeve
he is steered to a seat, led by the lord
who greets Gawain by name as his guest.
No man in the world is more welcome, are his words.
For that he is thanked. And they hug there and then
940 and sit as a pair through the service in prayer.
Then she who desired to see this stranger
came from her closet with her sisterly crew.
She was fairest amongst them—her face, her flesh,
her complexion, her quality, her bearing, her body,

And wener then Wenore, as the wyye thoght,
He ches thurgh the chaunsel, to cheryche that hende.
An other lady hir lad bi the lyft honde,
That was alder then ho, an auncian hit semed,
And heghly honowred with hatheles aboute.
950 Bot unlyke on to loke tho ladyes were,
For if the yonge was yep, yolwe was that other:
Riche red on that on rayled ayquere,
Rugh ronkled chekes that other on rolled.
Kerchofes of that on, wyth mony cler perles,
Hir brest and hir bryght throte bare displayed
Schon schyrer then snawe that schedes on hilles;
That other wyth a gorger was gered over the swyre,
Chymbled over hir blake chyn with chalk-quyte vayles,
Hir frount folden in sylk, enfoubled ayquere,
960 Toret and treleted with tryfles aboute,
That noght was bare of that burde bot the blake browes,
The tweyne yyen and the nase, the naked lyppes,
And those were soure to se and sellyly blered—
A mensk lady on molde mon may hir calle,
                    for Gode!
            Hir body was schort and thik,
            Hir buttokes bay and brode;
            More lykkerwys on to lyk
            Was that scho hade on lode.

970 When Gawayn glyght on that gay that graciously loked,
Wyth leve laght of the lorde he went hem ayaynes.
The alder he haylses, heldande ful lowe;
The loveloker he lappes a lyttel in armes,
He kysses hir comlyly and knyghtly he meles.
Thay kallen hym of aquoyntaunce, and he hit quyk askes

more glorious than Guinevere, or so Gawain thought,
and in the chancel of the church they exchanged courtesies.
She was hand in hand with a lady to her left,
someone altered by age, an ancient dame,
well respected, it seemed, by the servants at her side.

950 Those ladies were not the least bit alike:
one woman was young, one withered by years.
The body of the beauty seemed to bloom with blood,
the cheeks of the crone were wattled and slack.
One was clothed in a kerchief clustered with pearls
which shone like snow—snow on the slopes
of her upper breast and bright bare throat.
The other was noosed and knotted at the neck,
her chin enveloped in chalk-white veils,
her forehead fully enfolded in silk

960 with detailed designs at the edges and hems;
nothing bare, except for the black of her brows
and the eyes and nose and naked lips
which were chapped and bleared and a sorrowful sight.
A grand old mother, a matriarch she might
         be hailed.
      Her trunk was square and squat,
      her buttocks bulged and swelled.
      Most men would sooner squint
      at her whose hand she held.

970 Then Gawain glanced at the gracious-looking woman,
and by leave of the lord he approached those ladies
saluting the elder with a long, low bow,
holding the other for a moment in his arms,
kissing her respectfully and speaking with courtesy.
They request his acquaintance, and quickly he offers

To be her servaunt sothly, if hemself lyked.

Thay tan hym bytwene hem, wyth talkyng hym leden

To chambre, to chemné, and chefly thay asken

Spyces, that unsparely men speded hom to bryng,

980 And the wynnelych wyne therwith uche tyme.

The lorde luflych aloft lepes ful ofte,

Mynned merthe to be made upon mony sythes,

Hent heghly of his hode, and on a spere henged,

And wayned hom to wynne the worchip therof

That most myrthe myght meve that Crystenmas whyle.

"And I schal fonde, bi my fayth, to fylter wyth the best

Er me wont the wede, with help of my frendes."

Thus wyth laghande lotes the lorde hit tayt makes,

For to glade Sir Gawayn with gomnes in halle

990   that nyght,

            Til that hit was tyme

            The lorde comaundet lyght.

            Sir Gawen his leve con nyme

            And to his bed hym dight.

On the morne, as uch mon mynes that tyme

That dryghtyn for oure destyné to deye was borne,

Wele waxes in uche a won in worlde for his sake.

So did hit there on that day thurgh dayntés mony:

Bothe at mes and at mele messes ful quaynt

1000 Derf men upon dece drest of the best.

The olde auncian wyf heghest ho syttes;

The lorde lufly her by lent, as I trowe.

Gawan and the gay burde togeder thay seten

Even inmyddes, as the messe metely come;

And sythen thurgh al the sale, as hem best semed,

Bi uche grome at his degré graythely was served.

to serve them unswervingly should they say the word.
They take him between them and talk as they walk
to a hearth full of heat, and hurriedly ask
for specially spiced cakes, which are speedily fetched,
980 and wine filled each goblet again and again.
Frequently the lord would leap to his feet
insisting that mirth and merriment be made:
hauling off his hood he hoisted it on a spear—
a prize, he promised, to the person providing
most comfort and cheer at Christmastime.
"And my fellows and friends shall help in my fight
to see that it hangs from no head but my own."
So the laughter of that lord lights up the room,
and Gawain and the gathering are gladdened by games
990   till late.
            So late, his lordship said,
            that lamps should burn with light.
            Then, blissful, bound for bed,
            Sir Gawain waved good night.

So the morning dawns when man remembers
the day our Redeemer was born to die,
and every house on earth is joyful for Lord Jesus.
Their day was no different, being a diary of delights:
banquets and buffets were beautifully cooked
1000 and dutifully served to diners at the dais.
The ancient elder sat highest at the table
with the lord, I believe, in the chair to her left;
the sweeter one and Gawain took seats in the center
and were first at the feast to dine, then food
was carried around as custom decrees
and served to each man as his status deserved.

Ther was mete, ther was myrthe, ther was much joye,

That for to telle therof hit me tene were,

And to poynte hit yet I pyned me paraventure.

1010 Bot yet I wot that Wawen and the wale burde

Such comfort of her compaynye caghten togeder

Thurgh her dere dalyaunce of her derne wordes,

Wyth clene cortays carp closed fro fylthe,

That hor play was passande uche prynce gomen,

    in vayres.

    Trumpes and nakerys,

    Much pypyng ther repayres;

    Uche mon tented hys,

    And thay two tented thayres.

1020 Much dut was ther dryven that day and that other,

And the thryd as thro thronge in therafter;

The joye of sayn Jones day was gentyle to here,

And was the last of the layk, leudes ther thoghten.

Ther wer gestes to go upon the gray morne,

Forthy wonderly thay woke, and the wyn dronken,

Daunsed ful dreyly wyth dere caroles.

At the last, when hit was late, thay lachen her leve,

Uchon to wende on his way that was wyye strange.

Gawan gef hym god day, the godmon hym lachches,

1030 Ledes hym to his awen chambre, the chymné bysyde,

And there he drawes hym on dryye, and derely hym thonkkes

Of the wynne worschip that he hym wayved hade,

As to honour his hous on that hyghe tyde,

And enbelyse his burgh with his bele chere.

"Iwysse, sir, quyl I leve, me worthes the better

That Gawayn has ben my gest at Goddes awen fest."

"Grant merci, sir," quoth Gawayn, "in god fayth hit is yowres,

There was feasting, there was fun, and such feelings of joy
as could not be conveyed by quick description,
yet to tell it in detail would take too much time.
1010 But I'm aware that Gawain and the beautiful woman
found such comfort and closeness in each other's company
through warm exchanges of whispered words
and refined conversation free from foulness
that their pleasure surpassed all princely sports
by far.
Beneath the din of drums
men followed their affairs,
and trumpets thrilled and thrummed
as those two tended theirs.

1020 They drank and danced all day and the next
and danced and drank the day after that,
then Saint John's Day passed with a gentler joy
as the Christmas feasting came to a close.
Guests were to go in the grayness of dawn,
so they laughed and dined as the dusk darkened,
swaying and swirling to music and song.
Then at last, in the lateness, they upped and left
toward distant parts along different paths.
Gawain offered his good-byes, but was ushered by his host
1030 to his host's own chamber and the heat of its chimney,
waylaid by the lord so the lord might thank him
profoundly and profusely for the favor he had shown
in honoring his house at that hallowed season
and lighting every corner of the castle with his character.
"For as long as I live my life shall be better
that Gawain was my guest at God's own feast."
"By God," said Gawain, "but the gratitude goes to you.

Al the honour is your awen—the heghe kyng yow yelde!
And I am, wyye, at your wylle, to worch youre hest,
As I am halden therto, in hyghe and in lowe,
              bi right."
          The lorde fast can hym payne
          To holde lenger the knyght;
          To hym answres Gawayn
          Bi non way that he myght.

Then frayned the freke ful fayre at himselven
Quat derve dede had hym dryven at that dere tyme
So kenly fro the kynges kourt to kayre al his one,
Er the halidayes holly were halet out of toun.
"For sothe, sir," quoth the segge, "ye sayn bot the trawthe,
A heghe ernde and a hasty me hade fro tho wones,
For I am sumned myselfe to sech to a place,
I ne wot in worlde whederwarde to wende hit to fynde.
I nolde bot if I hit negh myght on Nw Yeres morne
For alle the londe inwyth Logres, so me oure Lorde help!
Forthy, sir, this enquest I require yow here,
That ye me telle with trawthe if ever ye tale herde
Of the grene chapel, quere hit on grounde stondes,
And of the knyght that hit kepes, of colour of grene.
Ther was stabled bi statut a steven uus bytwene
To mete that mon at that mere, yif I myght last;
And of that ilk Nw Yere bot neked now wontes,
And I wolde loke on that lede, if God me let wolde,
Gladloker, bi Goddes Sun, then any god welde.
Forthi, iwysse, bi yowre wylle, wende me bihoves.
Naf I now to busy bot bare thre dayes,
And me als fayn to falle feye as fayly of myyn ernde."
Thenne laghande quoth the lorde: "Now leng the byhoves,

May the High King of Heaven repay your honor.
Your requests are now this knight's commands.
1040 I am bound by your bidding, no boon is too high
　　　　　to say."
　　　　At length his lordship tried
　　　　to get his guest to stay.
　　　　But proud Gawain replied
　　　　he must now make his way.

Then the lord, being curious, made a courteous inquiry
of what desperate deed in the depth of winter
should coax him from Camelot, so quickly and alone,
before Christmas was over in his king's court.
1050 "What you ask," said the knight, "you shall now know.
A most pressing matter prized me from that place:
I myself am summoned to seek out a site
and I have not the faintest idea where to find it.
But find it I must by the first of the year, and not fail
for all the acres in England, so help me Lord.
And in speaking of my quest, I respectfully request
that you tell me, in truth, if you have heard the tale
of a green chapel, or the grounds where a Green Chapel stands,
or the guardian of those grounds who is colored green.
1060 For I am bound by a bond agreed by us both
to link up with him there, should I live that long.
As dawn on New Year's Day draws near,
if God sees fit, I shall face that freak
more happily than I would the most wondrous wealth!
With your blessing, therefore, I must follow my feet.
In three short days my destiny is due,
and I would rather drop dead than default from duty."
Then laughing out loud the lord said, "Relax!

For I schal teche yow to that terme bi the tymes ende.
1070 The grene chapayle upon grounde greve yow no more;
Bot ye schal be in yowre bed, burne, at thyn ese,
Quyle forth dayes, and ferk on the fyrst of the yere,
And cum to that merk at mydmorn, to make quat yow likes
            in spenne.
        Dowelles whyle New Yeres daye,
        And rys and raykes thenne.
        Mon schal yow sette in waye;
        Hit is not two myle henne."

Thenne was Gawan ful glad, and gomenly he laghed:
1080 "Now I thonk yow thryvandely thurgh alle other thynge;
Now acheved is my chaunce, I schal at your wylle
Dowelle, and elles do quat ye demen."
Thenne sesed hym the syre and set hym bysyde,
Let the ladies be fette, to lyke hem the better.
Ther was scmc solace by hemself stille.
The lorde let for luf lotes so myry,
As wyy that wolde of his wyte, ne wyst quat he myght.
Thenne he carped to the knyght, criande loude:
"Ye han demed to do the dede that I bidde.
1090 Wyl ye halde this hes here at thys ones?"
"Ye, sir, for sothe," sayd the segge trwe,
"Whyl I byde in yowre borghe, be bayn to yowre hest."
"For ye haf travayled," quoth the tulk, "towen fro ferre,
And sythen waked me wyth, ye arn not wel waryst
Nauther of sostnaunce ne of slepe, sothly I knowe.
Ye schal lenge in your lofte and lyye in your ese
To-morn quyle the messe-quyle, and to mete wende
When ye wyl, wyth my wyf, that wyth yow schal sitte

I'll direct you to your rendezvous when the time is right,

1070 you'll get to the green chapel, so give up your grieving.

You can bask in your bed, bide your time,

save your fond farewells till the first of the year

and still meet him by midmorning to do as you may.

         So stay.

      A guide will get you there

      at dawn on New Year's Day.

      The place you need is near,

      two miles at most away."

Then Gawain was giddy with gladness, and declared,

1080 "For this more than anything I thank you thoroughly.

Now my sight is set, and I'll stay in your service

until that time, attending every task."

The lord squeezed Gawain's arm and seated him at his side,

and called for the ladies to keep them company.

There was pleasure aplenty in their private talk:

the lips of the lord ran wild with words,

like the mouth of a madman, not knowing his own mind.

Then speaking to Gawain, he suddenly shouted:

"You have sworn to serve me, whatever I instruct.

1090 Will you hold to that oath right here and now?"

"You may trust my tongue," said Gawain, in truth,

"for within these walls I am servant to your will."

The lord said warmly, "You were weary and worn,

hollow with hunger, harrowed by tiredness,

yet you joined in my reveling right royally every night.

You relax as you like, lie in your bed

until mass tomorrow, then go to your meal

where my wife will be waiting; she will sit at your side

And comfort yow with compayny, til I to cort torne.

1100   Ye lende,

And I schal erly ryse;

On huntyng wyl I wende."

Gauayn grantes alle thyse,

Hym heldande, as the hende.

"Yet firre," quoth the freke, "a forwarde we make:

Quat-so-ever I wynne in the wod, hit worthes to youres;

And quat chek so ye acheve, chaunge me therforne.

Swete, swap we so—sware with trawthe—

Quether, leude, so lymp lere other better."

1110   "Bi God," quoth Gawayn the gode, "I grant thertylle,

And that yow lyst for to layke, lef hit me thynkes."

"Who brynges uus this beverage, this bargayn is maked,"

So sayde the lorde of that lede. Thay laghed uchone,

Thay dronken and daylyeden and dalten untyghtel,

Thise lordes and ladyes, quyle that hem lyked;

And sythen with frenkysch fare and fele fayre lotes

Thay stoden and stemed and stylly speken,

Kysten ful comlyly and kaghten her leve.

With mony leude ful lyght and lemande torches,

1120 Uche burne to his bed was broght at the laste

                    ful softe.

            To bed yet er thay yede,

            Recorded covenauntes ofte;

            The olde lorde of that leude

            Cowthe wel halde layk alofte.

to accompany and comfort you in my absence from court.

1100 　　　　　So lounge:
　　　at dawn I'll rise and ride
　　　to hunt with horse and hound."
　　　The gracious knight agreed
　　　and, bending low, he bowed.

"Furthermore," said the master, "let's make a pact.
Here's a wager: what I win in the woods will be yours,
and what you gain while I'm gone you will give to me.
Young sir, let's swap, and strike a bond,
let a bargain be a bargain, for worse or for better."
1110 "By God," said Gawain, "I agree to the terms,
and I find it pleasing that you favor such fun."
"Let drink be served and we'll seal the deal,"
the lord cried loudly, and everyone laughed.
So they reveled and caroused uproariously,
those lords and ladies, for as long as they liked,
then they tired and they slowed and they stood and they spoke
with immaculate exchanges of manners and remarks.
And with parting kisses the party dispersed,
footmen going forward with flaring torches,
1120 and every lord was led at last towards bed,
　　　　　to dream.
　　　Before they part the pair
　　　repeat their pact again.
　　　That lord was well aware
　　　of how to host a game.

III

Ful erly bifore the day the folk up rysen;
Gestes that go wolde hor gromes thay calden,
And thay busken up bilyve blonkkes to sadel,
Tyffen her takles, trussen her males.
1130 Richen hem the rychest, to ryde alle arayde,
Lepen up lyghtly, lachen her brydeles,
Uche wyye on his way ther hym wel lyked.
The leve lorde of the londe was not the last
Arayed for the rydyng, with renkkes ful mony;
Ete a sop hastyly, when he hade herde masse,
With bugle to bent-felde he buskes bylyve.
By that any daylyght lemed upon erthe.
He with his hatheles on hyghe horsses weren.
Thenne thise cacheres that couthe cowpled hor houndes,
1140 Unclosed the kenel dore and calde hem theroute,
Blwe bygly in bugles thre bare motes;
Braches bayed therfore and breme noyse maked,
And thay chastysed and charred on chasyng that went,
A hundreth of hunteres, as I haf herde telle,
　　　　　　of the best.
　　　　To trystors vewters yod,
　　　　Couples huntes of kest;
　　　　Ther ros for blastes gode
　　　　Gret rurd in that forest.

FITT III

Well before sunrise the servants were stirring;
the guests who were going had called for their grooms
and they scurried to the stables to ready the steeds,
trussing and tying all the trammel and tack.
1130   The high-ranking nobles got ready to ride,
jumped stylishly to their saddles and seized the reins,
then cantered away on their chosen courses.
The lord of that land was by no means last
to be rigged out for riding with the rest of his men.
After mass he wolfed down a meal, then made
for the hunting grounds with his hunting horn.
So as morning was lifting its lamp to the land
his lordship and his huntsmen were high on horseback,
and the canny kennel men had coupled the hounds
1140   and opened the cages and called them out.
On the bugles they blew three bellowing notes
to a din of baying and barking, and the dogs
which chased or wandered were chastened by whip.
As I heard it, we're talking a hundred top hunters
                at least.
          The handlers hold their hounds,
          the huntsmen's hounds run free.
          Each bugle blast rebounds
          between the trunks of trees.

1150   At the fyrst quethe of the quest quaked the wylde;

Der drof in the dale, doted for drede,

Hiyed to the hyghe, bot heterly thay were

Restayed with the stablye, that stoutly ascryed.

Thay let the herttes haf the gate, with the hyghe hedes,

The breme bukkes also with hor brode paumes;

For the fre lorde hade defende in fermysoun tyme

That ther schulde no mon meve to the male dere.

The hindes were halden in with "hay!" and "war!"

The does dryven with gret dyn to the depe slades.

1160   Ther myght mon se, as thay slypte, slentyng of arwes;

At uche wende under wande wapped a flone,

That bigly bote on the broun with ful brode hedes.

What! thay brayen and bleden, bi bonkkes thay deyen,

And ay rachches in a res radly hem folwes,

Hunteres wyth hyghe horne hasted hem after,

Wyth such a crakkande kry as klyffes haden brusten.

What wylde so atwaped wyyes that schotten

Was al toraced and rent at the resayt,

Bi thay were tened at the hyghe and taysed to the wattres.

1170   The ledes were so lerned at the lowe trysteres,

And the grehoundes so grete, that geten hem bylyve

And hem tofylched as fast as frekes myght loke,

           ther ryght.

        The lorde for blys abloy

        Ful oft con launce and lyght,

        And drof that day wyth joy

        Thus to the derk nyght.

Thus laykes this lorde by lynde-wodes eves,

And Gawayn the god mon in gay bed lyges,

1180   Lurkkes quyl the daylyght lemed on the wowes,

1150 As the cry went up the wild creatures quaked.
The deer in the dale, quivering with dread
hurtled to high ground, but were headed off
by the ring of beaters who bawled and roared.
The stags of the herd with their high-branched heads
and the broad-horned bucks were allowed to pass by,
for the lord of the land had laid down a law
that man should not maim the male in close season.
But the hinds were halted with hollers and whoops
and the din drove the does to sprint for the dells.
1160 Then the eye can see that the air is all arrows:
all across the forest they flashed and flickered,
biting through hides with their broad heads.
What! They bleat as they bleed and they die on the banks,
and always the hounds are hard on their heels,
and the hunters on horseback come hammering behind
with stone-splitting cries, as if cliffs had collapsed.
And those animals which escaped the aim of the archers
were steered from the slopes down to rivers and streams
and set upon and seized at the stations below.
1170 So perfect and practiced were the men at their posts
and so great were the greyhounds which grappled with the deer
that prey was pounced on and dispatched with speed
                and force.
          The lord's heart leaps with life.
          Now on, now off his horse
          all day he hacks and drives.
          And dusk comes in due course.

So through a lime-leaf border the lord led the hunt,
while snug in his sheets lay slumbering Gawain,
1180 dozing as the daylight dappled the walls,

Under covertour ful clere, cortyned aboute.

And as in slomeryng he slode, sleyly he herde

A littel dyn at his dor, and derfly upon;

And he heves up his hed out of the clothes,

A corner of the cortyn he caght up a lyttel,

And waytes warly thiderwarde quat hit be myght.

Hit was the ladi, loflyest to beholde,

That drow the dor after hir ful dernly and stylle,

And bowed towarde the bed; and the burne schamed,

1190   And layde hym doun lystyly and let as he slepte.

And ho stepped stilly and stel to his bedde,

Kest up the cortyn and creped withinne,

And set hir ful softly on the bed-syde

And lenged there selly longe, to loke quen he wakened.

The lede lay lurked a ful longe quyle,

Compast in his concience to quat that cace myght

Meve other amount, to mervayle hym thoght.

Bot yet he saydc in hymself: "More semly hit were

To aspye wyth my spelle in space quat ho wolde."

1200   Then he wakenede and wroth and to-hir-warde torned,

And unlouked his yye-lyddes and let as hym wondered,

And sayned hym, as bi his sawe the saver to worthe,

> with hande.

>> Wyth chynne and cheke ful swete,

>> Bothe quit and red in blande,

>> Ful lufly con ho lete,

>> Wyth lyppes smal laghande.

"God moroun, Sir Gawayn," sayde that gay lady,

"Ye ar a sleper unslyye, that mon may slyde hider.

1210   Now ar ye tan astyt, bot true uus may schape,

I schal bynde yow in your bedde, that be ye trayst."

under a splendid cover, enclosed by curtains.
And while snoozing he heard a slyly made sound,
the sigh of a door swinging slowly aside.
From below the bedding he brings up his head
and lifts the corner of the curtain a little
wondering warily what it might be.
It was she, the lady, looking her loveliest,
most quietly and craftily closing the door,
nearing the bed. The knight felt nervous;
1190 lying back he assumed the shape of sleep
as she stole towards him with silent steps,
then clasped the curtain and crept inside,
then sat down softly at the side of his bed.
And awaited him wakening for a good long while.
Gawain lay still, in his state of false sleep,
turning over in his mind what this matter might mean,
and where the lady's unlikely visit might lead.
Yet he said to himself, "Instead of this stealth
I should openly ask what her actions imply."
1200 So he stirred and stretched, turned on his side,
lifted his eyelids and, looking alarmed,
signed himself hurriedly with his hand, as if saving
        his life.
      Her chin is pale, her cheeks
      are ruddy red with health;
      her smile is sweet, she speaks
      with lips that love to laugh:

"Good morning, Sir Gawain," said the graceful lady,
"You sleep so soundly one might sidle in here.
1210 You're tricked and you're trapped! But let's make a truce,
or I'll besiege you in your bed, and you'd better believe me."

Al laghande the lady lauced tho bourdes.

"Goud moroun, gay," quoth Gawayn the blythe,

"Me schal worthe at your wille, and that me wel lykes,

For I yelde me yederly and yeye after grace;

And that is the best, be my dome, for me byhoves nede."

And thus he bourded ayayn with mony a blythe laghter.

"Bot wolde ye, lady lovely, then leve me grante,

And deprece your prysoun and pray hym to ryse,

1220 I wolde bowe of this bed and busk me better,

I schulde kever the more comfort to karp yow wyth."

"Nay, for sothe, beau sir," sayd that swete,

"Ye schal not rise of your bedde. I rych yow better:

I schal happe yow here that other half als,

And sythen karp wyth my knyght that I kaght have;

For I wene wel, iwysse, Sir Wowen ye are,

That alle the worlde worchipes, quere-so ye ride.

Your honour, your hendelayk is hendely praysed

With lordes, wyth ladyes, with alle that lyf bere.

1230 And now ye ar here, iwysse, and we bot oure one;

My lorde and his ledes ar on lenthe faren,

Other burnes in her bedde, and my burdes als,

The dor drawen and dit with a derf haspe.

And sythen I have in this hous hym that al lykes,

I schal ware my whyle wel, quyl hit lastes,

         with tale.

      Ye ar welcum to my cors,

      Yowre awen won to wale;

      Me behoves of fyne force

1240   Your servaunt be, and schale."

"In god fayth," quoth Gawayn, "gayn hit me thynkkes,

Thagh I be not now he that ye of speken;

She giggled girlishly as she teased good Gawain.
The man in the bed said, "Good morning, ma'am.
I'll contentedly attend whatever task you set,
and in serving your desires I shall seek your mercy,
which seems my best plan, in the circumstances!"
And he loaded his light-hearted words with laughter.
"But my gracious lady, if you grant me leave,
will you pardon this prisoner and prompt him to rise,
1220   then I'll quit these covers and pull on my clothes,
and our words will flow more freely back and forth."
"Not so, beautiful sir," the sweet lady said.
"Bide in your bed—my own plan is better.
I'll tuck in your covers corner to corner,
then playfully parley with the man I have pinned.
Because I know your name—the knight Sir Gawain,
famed through the realm whichever road he rides,
whose princely honor is highly praised
amongst lords and ladies and everyone alive.
1230   And right here you lie. And we are left all alone,
with my husband and his huntsmen away in the hills
and the servants snoring and my maids asleep
and the door to this bedroom barred with a bolt.
I have in my house an honored guest
so I'll take my time; I'll be talking to him for
                a while.
        You're free to have my all,
        do with me what you will.
        I'll come just as you call
1240   and swear to serve you well."

"In good faith," said Gawain, "such gracious flattery,
though in truth I'm not nearly such a noble knight.

To reche to such reverence as ye reherce here

I am wyye unworthy, I wot wel myselven.

Bi God, I were glad and yow god thoght

At sawe other at servyce that I sette myght

To the plesaunce of your prys—hit were a pure joye."

"In god fayth, Sir Gawayn," quoth the gay lady,

"The prys and the prowes that pleses al other,

1250   If I hit lakked other set at lyght, hit were littel daynté;

Bot hit ar ladyes innoghe that lever wer nowthe

Haf the, hende, in hor holde, as I the habbe here,

To daly with derely your daynté wordes,

Kever hem comfort and colen her cares,

Then much of the garysoun other golde that thay haven.

Bot I louve that ilk lorde that the lyfte haldes,

I haf hit holly in my honde that al desyres,

               thurghe grace."

        Scho made hym so gret chere,

1260   That was so fayr of face;

        The knyght with speches skere

        Answared to uche a cace.

"Madame," quoth the myry mon, "Mary yow yelde,

For I haf founden, in god fayth, yowre fraunchis nobele.

And other ful much of other folk fongen hor dedes,

Bot the daynté that thay delen for my disert nysen.

Hit is the worchyp of yourself that noght bot wel connes."

"Bi Mary," quoth the menskful, "me thynk hit another;

For were I worth al the wone of wymmen alyve,

1270   And al the wele of the worlde were in my honde,

And I schulde chepen and chose to cheve me a lorde,

For the costes that I haf knowen upon the, knyght, here,

Of bewté and debonerté and blythe semblaunt,

I don't dare to receive the respect you describe
and in no way warrant such worthy words.
But by God, I'd be glad, if you give me the right,
to serve your desires, and with action or speech
bring you perfect pleasure. The honor would be priceless."
Said the gracious lady, "Sir Gawain, in good faith,
how improper on my part if I were to imply
1250   any slur or slight on your status as a knight.
But what lady in this land wouldn't latch the door,
wouldn't rather hold you as I do here—
in the company of your clever conversation,
forgetting all grief and engaging in joy—
than hug to her heart a horde of gold?
I praise the Lord who upholds the high heavens,
for I have what I hoped for above all else by
                    his grace."
                That lovely looking maid,
1260   she charmed him and she chased.
                But every move she made
                he countered, case by case.

"Madam," said our man, "may Mary bless you,
in good faith, you are kind and the fairest of the fair.
Some fellows are praised for the feats they perform;
I hardly deserve to receive such respect,
whereas you are genuinely joyful and generous."
"By Mary," she declared, "it's quite the contrary.
Were I the wealthiest woman in the world
1270   with priceless pearls in the palm of my hand
to bargain with and buy the best of all men,
then for all the signs you have shown me, sir,
of kindness, courtesy and exquisite looks—

And that I haf er herkkened and halde hit here trwee,
Ther schulde no freke upon folde bifore yow be chosen."
"Iwysse, worthy," quoth the wyye, "ye haf waled wel better;
Bot I am proude of the prys that ye put on me,
And, soberly your servaunt, my soverayn I holde yow,
And yowre knyght I becom, and Kryst yow foryelde!"
1280 Thus thay meled of muchquat til mydmorn paste,
And ay the lady let lyk a hym loved mych;
The freke ferde with defence, and feted ful fayre.
"Thagh I were burde bryghtest," the burde in mynde hade,
"The lasse luf in his lode"—for lur that he soght
             boute hone,
        The dunte that schulde hym deve,
        And nedes hit most be done.
        The lady thenn spek of leve,
        He granted hir ful sone.

1290 Thenne ho gef hym god day, and wyth a glent laghed,
And as ho stod ho stonyed hym wyth ful stor wordes;
"Now he that spedes uche spech this disport yelde yow!
Bot that ye be Gawan, hit gos not in mynde."
"Querfore?" quoth the freke, and freschly he askes,
Ferde lest he hade fayled in fourme of his costes.
Bot the burde hym blessed, and bi this skyl sayde:
"So god as Gawayn gaynly is halden,
And cortaysye is closed so clene in hymselven,
Couth not lyghtly haf lenged so long wyth a lady,
1300 Bot he had craved a cosse bi his courtaysye,
Bi sum towch of summe tryfle at sum tales ende."
Then quoth Wowen: "Iwysse, worthe as yow lykes;
I schal kysse at your comaundement, as a knyght falles,
And firre, lest he displese yow, so plede hit no more."

a picture of perfection now proved to be true—
no person on this planet would be picked before you."
"In fairness," said Gawain, "you found far better.
But I'm proud of the price you would pay from your purse,
and will swear to serve you as my sovereign forever.
Let Christ now know that Gawain is your knight."
1280 Then they muse on many things through morning and midday,
and the lady stares with a loving look,
but Gawain is a gentleman and remains on guard,
and although no woman could be warmer or more winning,
he is cool in his conduct, on account of the scene he
    foresees:
        the strike he must receive,
        as cruel fate decrees.
        The lady begs her leave—
        at once Gawain agrees.

1290 She glanced at him, laughed and gave her good-bye,
then stood, and stunned him with astounding words:
"May the Lord repay you for your prize performance.
But I know that Gawain could never be your name."
"But why not?" asked the knight, in need of an answer,
afraid that some fault in his manners had failed him.
The beautiful woman blessed him, then rebuked him:
"A good man like Gawain, so greatly regarded,
the embodiment of courtliness to the bones of his being,
could never have lingered so long with a lady
1300 without craving a kiss, as politeness requires,
or coaxing a kiss with his closing words."
"Very well," said Gawain, "let's do as you wish.
If a kiss is your request I shall keep my promise
faithfully to fulfil you, so ask no further."

Ho comes nerre with that, and caches hym in armes,
Loutes luflych adoun and the leude kysses.
Thay comly bykennen to Kryst ayther other;
Ho dos hir forth at the dore withouten dyn more;
And he ryches hym to ryse and rapes hym sone,
1310 Clepes to his chamberlayn, choses his wede,
Bowes forth, quen he was boun, blythely to masse.
And thenne he meved to his mete that menskly hym keped,
And made myry al day til the mone rysed,
              with game.
            Was never freke fayrer fonge
            Bitwene two so dyngne dame,
            The alder and the yonge;
            Much solace set thay same.

And ay the lorde of the londe is lent on his gamnes,
1320 To hunt in holtes and hethe at hyndes barayne.
Such a sowme he ther slowe bi that the sunne heldet,
Of dos and of other dere, to deme were wonder.
Thenne fersly thay flokked in, folk at the laste,
And quykly of the quelled dere a querré thay maked.
The best bowed therto with burnes innoghe,
Gedered the grattest of gres that ther were,
And didden hem derely undo as the dede askes.
Serched hem at the asay summe that ther were,
Two fyngeres thay fonde of the fowlest of alle.
1330 Sythen thay slyt the slot, sesed the erber,
Schaved wyth a scharp knyf, and the schyre knitten.
Sythen rytte thay the foure lymmes and rent of the hyde,
Then brek thay the balé, the boweles out token
Lystily, for laucyng and lere of the knot.
Thay gryped to the gargulun, and graythely departed

The lady comes close, cradles him in her arms,
leans nearer and nearer, then kisses the knight.
Then they courteously commend one another to Christ,
and without one more word the woman is away.
He leaps from where he lies at a heck of a lick,
1310　calls for his chamberlain, chooses his clothes,
makes himself ready then marches off to mass.
Then he went to a meal which was made and waiting,
and was merry and amused till the moon had silvered
　　　　　　the view.
　　　　　No man felt more at home
　　　　　tucked in between those two,
　　　　　the cute one and the crone.
　　　　　Their gladness grew and grew.

And the lord of the land still led the hunt,
1320　driving hinds to their death through holts and heaths,
and by the setting of the sun had slaughtered so many
of the does and other deer that it beggared belief.
Then finally the folk came flocking to one spot
and quickly they collected and counted the kill.
Then the leading lords and their left-hand men
chose the finest deer—those fullest with fat—
and ordered them cut open by those skilled in the art.
They assessed and sized every slain creature
and even on the feeblest found two fingers worth of fat.
1330　Through the sliced-open throat they seized the stomach
and the butchered innards were bound in a bundle.
Next they lopped off the legs and peeled back the pelt
and hooked out the bowels through the broken belly,
but carefully, being cautious not to cleave the knot.
Then they clasped the throat, and clinically they cut

The wesaunt fro the wynt-hole and walt out the guttes.

Then scher thay out the schulderes with her scharp knyves,

Haled hem by a lyttel hole, to have hole sydes.

Sithen britned thay the brest and brayden hit in twynne.

1340 And eft at the gargulun bigynes on thenne,

Ryves hit up radly ryght to the byght,

Voydes out the avanters, and verayly therafter

Alle the rymes by the rybbes radly thay lauce.

So ryde thay of by resoun bi the rygge bones

Evenden to the haunche, that henged alle samen,

And heven hit up al hole and hwen hit of there.

And that thay neme for the noumbles bi nome, as I trowe,

bi kynde.

Bi the byght al of the thyghes

1350 The lappes thay lauce bihynde;

To hewe hit in two thay hyyes,

Bi the bakbon to unbynde.

Bothe the hede and the hals thay hwen of thenne,

And sythen sunder thay the sydes swyft fro the chyne,

And the corbeles fee thay kest in a greve.

Thenn thurled thay ayther thik side thurgh bi the rybbe,

And henged thenne ayther bi hoghes of the fourches,

Uche freke for his fee as falles for to have.

Upon a felle of the fayre best fede thay thayr houndes

1360 Wyth the lyver and the lyghtes, the lether of the paunches,

And bred bathed in blod blende ther-amonges.

Baldely thay blw prys, bayed thayr rachches;

Sythen fonge thay her flesche folden to home,

Strakande ful stoutly mony stif motes.

Bi that the daylyght was done, the douthe was al wonen

the gullet from the windpipe, then garbaged the guts.
Then the shoulder blades were severed with sharp knives
and slotted through a slit so the hide stayed whole.
Then the beasts were prized apart at the breast,
1340 and they went to work on the gralloching again,
riving open the front as far as the hind fork,
fetching out the offal, then with further purpose
filleting the ribs in the recognized fashion.
And the spine was subject to a similar process,
being pared to the haunch so it held as one piece
then hoisting it high and hacking it off.
And its name is the numbles, as far as I know, and
        just that.
      Its hind legs pulled apart
1350   they slit the fleshy flaps,
     then cleave and quickly start
     to break it down its back.

Then the heads and necks of hinds were hewn off,
and the choice meat of the flanks chopped away from the chine,
and a fee for the crows was cast into the copse.
Then each side was skewered, stabbed through the ribs
and heaved up high, hung by its hocks,
and every person was paid with appropriate portions.
Using pelts for plates, the dogs pogged out
1360 on liver and lights and stomach linings
and a blended sop of blood and bread.
The kill horn was blown and the bloodhounds bayed.
Then hauling their meat they headed for home,
sounding howling wails on their hunting horns,
and as daylight died they had covered the distance

Into the comly castel, ther the knyght bides

         ful stille,

     Wyth blys and bryght fyr bette.

     The lorde is comen thertylle;

1370   When Gawayn wyth hym mette,

     Ther was bot wele at wylle.

Thenne comaunded the lorde in that sale to samen alle the meny,

Bothe the ladyes on loghe to lyght with her burdes.

Bifore alle the folk on the flette, frekes he beddes

Verayly his venysoun to fech hym byforne;

And al godly in gomen Gawayn he called,

Teches hym to the tayles of ful tayt bestes,

Schewes hym the schyree grece schorne upon rybbes.

"How payes yow this play? Haf I prys wonnen?

1380 Have I thryvandely thonk thurgh my craft served?"

"Ye, iwysse," quoth that other wyye, "here is wayth fayrest

That I sey this seven yere in sesoun of wynter."

"And al I gif yow, Gawayn," quoth the gome thenne,

"For by acorde of covenaunt ye crave hit as your awen."

"This is soth," quoth the segge, "I say yow that ilke:

That I haf worthyly wonnen this wones wythinne,

Iwysse with as god wylle hit worthes to youres."

He hasppes his fayre hals his armes wythinne,

And kysses hym as comlyly as he couthe awyse:

1390 "Tas yow there my chevicaunce, I cheved no more;

I wowche hit saf fynly, thagh feler hit were."

"Hit is god," quoth the godmon, "grant mercy therfore.

Hit may be such, hit is the better and ye me breve wolde

Where ye wan this ilk wele bi wytte of yorselven."

"That was not forward," quoth he, "frayst me no more;

and were back in the abode where Gawain sat biding
his time.
Warm friends, warm flames will meet
the huntsman's home return.
1370   Gawain as well will greet
his host. Bright hearth fires burn.

Then the whole of the household was ordered to the hall,
and the women as well with their maids in waiting.
And once assembled he instructs the servants
that the venison be revealed in full view,
and in excellent humor he asked that Gawain
should see for himself the size of the kill,
and showed him the side slabs sliced from the ribs.
"Are you pleased with this pile? Have I won your praise?
1380 Does my skill at this sport deserve your esteem?"
"Why yes," said the other. "It's the hugest haul
I have seen, out of season, for several years."
"And I give it all to you, Gawain," said the master,
"for according to our contract it is yours to claim."
"Just so," said Gawain, "and I'll say the same,
for whatever I've won within these walls
such gains will be graciously given to you."
So he held out his arms and hugged the lord
and kissed him in the kindliest way he could.
1390 "You're welcome to my winnings—to my one profit,
though I'd gladly have given you any greater prize."
"I'm grateful," said the lord, "and Gawain, this gift
would carry more worth if you cared to confess
by what wit you won it. And when. And where."
"That wasn't our pact," he replied. "So don't pry.

For ye haf tan that yow tydes, trawe ye non other
               ye mowe."
          Thay laghed and made hem blythe
          Wyth lotes that were to lowe;
1400   To soper thay yede asswythe,
          Wyth dayntés nwe innowe.

And sythen by the chymné in chamber thay seten,
Wyyes the walle wyn weghed to hem oft,
And efte in her bourdyng thay baythen in the morn
To fylle the same forwardes that thay byfore maden:
That chaunce so bytydes, hor chevysaunce to chaunge,
What nwes so thay nome, at naght quen thay metten.
Thay acorded of the covenauntes byfore the court alle;
The beverage was broght forth in bourde at that tyme.
1410 Thenne thay lovelych leghten leve at the last,
Uche burne to his bedde busked bylyve.
Bi that the coke hade crowen and cakled bot thryse,
The lorde was lopen of his bedde, the leudes uch one,
So that the mete and the masse was metely delyvered,
The douthe dressed to the wod, er any day sprenged,
               to chace.
          Hegh with hunte and hornes
          Thurgh playnes thay passe in space,
          Uncoupled among tho thornes
1420   Raches that ran on race.

Sone thay calle of a quest in a ker syde,
The hunt rehayted the houndes that hit fyrst mynged,
Wylde wordes hym warp wyth a wrast noyce.
The howndes that hit herde hastid thider swythe,
And fellen as fast to the fuyt, fourty at ones.

You'll be given nothing greater, the agreement we have
                    holds good!"
            They laugh aloud and trade
            wise words which match their mood.
1400   When supper's meal is made
            they dine on dainty food.

Later, they lounged by the lord's fire,
and were served unstintingly with subtle wines
and agreed to the game again next morning
and to play by the rules already in place:
any takings to be traded between the two men
at night when they met, no matter what the merchandise.
They concurred on this contract in front of the court,
and drank on the deal, and went on drinking
1410 till late, when they took their leave at last,
and every person present disappeared to bed.
By the third cackle of the crowing cock
the lord and his liegemen are leaping from their beds,
and mass and the morning meal are taken,
and riders are rigged out ready to run as
                    day dawns.
            They leave the levels, loud
            with howling hunting horns.
            The huntsmen loose the hounds
1420   through thickets and through thorns.

Soon they picked up a scent at the side of a swamp
and the hounds which first found it were urged ahead
by a wild-voiced hunter and his wailing words.
The pack responded with vigor and pace,
alert to the trail, forty lurchers at least.

Thenne such a glaver ande glam of gedered rachches

Ros that the rocheres rungen aboute.

Hunteres hem hardened with horne and wyth muthe;

Then al in a semblé sweyed togeder

1430 Bitwene a flosche in that fryth and a foo cragge.

In a knot bi a clyffe, at the kerre syde,

Ther as the rogh rocher unrydely was fallen,

Thay ferden to the fyndyng, and frekes hem after.

Thay umbekesten the knarre and the knot bothe,

Wyyes, whyl thay wysten wel wythinne hem hit were,

The best that ther breved was wyth three blodhoundes.

Thenne thay beten on the buskes and bede hym up ryse.

And he unsoundyly out soght segges overthwert—

On the sellokest swyn swenged out there,

1440 Long sythen fro the sounder that synglere for olde,

For he was brothe, bor alther grattest,

Ful grymme quen he gronyed. Thenne greved mony,

For thre at the fyrst thrast he thryght to the erthe,

And sped hym forth good sped boute spyt more.

Thise other halowed "hyghe!" ful hyghe, and "hay! hay!" cryed,

Haden hornes to mouthe, heterly rechated.

Mony was the miyry mouthe of men and of houndes

That buskkes after this bor with bost and wyth noyse,

            to quelle.

1450   Ful oft he bydes the baye

          And maymes the mute inn melle;

          He hurtes of the houndes, and thay

          Ful yomerly yaule and yelle.

Schalkes to schote at hym schowen to thenne,

Haled to hym of her arewes, hitten hym oft;

Bot the poyntes payred at the pyth that pyght in his scheldes,

Then such a raucous din rose up all around them
it ricocheted and rang through the rocky slopes.
The hounds were mushed with hollers and the horn,
then suddenly they swerved and swarmed together
1430 in a wood, between a pool and a precipice.
On a mound, near a cliff, on the margins of a marsh
where toppled stones lay scattered and strewn
they coursed towards their quarry with huntsmen close at heel.
Then a crew of them ringed the hillock and the cliff,
until they were certain that inside their circle
was the beast whose being the bloodhounds had sensed.
Then they riled the creature with their rowdy ruckus,
and suddenly he breaks the barrier of beaters,
—the biggest of wild boars has bolted from his cover—
1440 ancient in years and estranged from the herd,
savage and strong, a most massive swine
with a fearsome grunt. And the group were disgruntled,
for three were thrown down by the first of his thrusts,
then he fled away fast before inflicting further damage.
The other huntsmen bawled "hi" and "hay, hay"
blasted on their bugles, blew to regroup,
so the dogs and the men made a merry din,
tracking him nosily, testing him time and time
                    again.
1450   The boar would stand at bay
              and aim to maul and maim
              the thronging dogs, and they
              would yelp and yowl in pain.

The front men stepped forward to fire a shot
aimed arrows at him which were often on target,
but their points could not pierce his impenetrable shoulders

And the barbes of his browe bite non wolde,

Thagh the schaven schaft schyndered in peces,

The hede hypped ayayn were-so-ever hit hitte.

1460 Bot quen the dyntes hym dered of her dryye strokes,

Then, braynwod for bate, on burnes he rases,

Hurtes hem ful heterly ther he forth hyyes,

And mony arwed therat and on lyte drowen.

Bot the lorde on a lyght horce launces hym after,

As burne bolde upon bent his bugle he blowes,

He rechated and rode thurgh rones ful thyk,

Suande this wylde swyn til the sunne schafted.

This day wyth this ilk dede thay dryven on this wyse,

Whyle oure luflych lede lys in his bedde,

1470 Gawayn graythely at home, in geres ful ryche

of hewe.

The lady noght foryate,

Com to hym to salue;

Ful erly ho was hym ate

His mode for to remwe.

Ho commes to the cortyn and at the knyght totes.

Sir Wawen her welcumed worthy on fyrst,

And ho hym yeldes ayayn ful yerne of hir wordes,

Settes hir sofly by his syde, and swythely ho laghes,

1480 And wyth a luflych loke ho layde hym thyse wordes:

"Sir, yif ye be Wawen, wonder me thynkkes,

Wyye that is so wel wrast alway to god,

And connes not of compaynye the costes undertake,

And if mon kennes yow hom to knowe, ye kest hom of your mynde.

Thou has foryeten yederly that yisterday I taghtte

Bi alder-truest token of talk that I cowthe."

"What is that?" quoth the wyghe, "iwysse I wot never.

and bounced away from his bristly brow.
The smooth, slender shafts splintered into pieces,
and the heads glanced away from wherever they hit.
1460 Battered and baited by such bombardment,
in frenzied fury he flies at the men,
hurts them horribly as he hurtles past
so that many grew timid and retreated a tad.
But the master of the manor gave chase on his mount,
the boldest of beast hunters, his bugle blaring,
trumpeting the tally-ho and tearing through thickets
till the setting sun slipped from the western sky.
So the day was spent in pursuits of this style,
while our lovable young lord had not left his bed,
1470 and, cosseted in costly quilted covers, there he
                    remained.
              The lady, at first light,
              did not neglect Gawain,
              but went to wake the knight
              and meant to change his mind.

She approaches the curtains, parts them and peeps in,
at which Sir Gawain makes her welcome at once,
and with prompt speech she replies to the prince,
settling by his side and giggling sweetly,
1480 looking at him lovingly before launching her words.
"If this is Gawain who greets me, I am galled
that a man so dedicated to doing his duty
cannot heed the first rule of honorable behavior,
which has entered through one ear and exited the other;
you have already lost what yesterday you learned
in the truest lesson my tongue could teach."
"What lesson?" asked the knight. "I know of none,

If hit be sothe that ye breve, the blame is myn awen."

"Yet I kende yow of kyssyng," quoth the clere thenne,

1490 "Quere-so countenaunce is couthe, quikly to clayme;

That bicumes uche a knyght that cortaysy uses."

"Do way," quoth that derf mon, "my dere, that speche,

For that durst I not do, lest I devayed were;

If I were werned, I were wrang, iwysse, yif I profered."

"Ma fay," quoth the mere wyf, "ye may not be werned;

Ye ar stif innoghe to constrayne wyth strenkthe, yif yow lykes,

Yif any were so vilanous that yow devaye wolde."

"Ye, be God," quoth Gawayn, "good is your speche,

Bot threte is unthryvande in thede ther I lende,

1500 And uche gift that is geven not with goud wylle.

I am at your comaundement, to kysse quen yow lykes;

Ye may lach quen yow lyst, and leve quen yow thynkkes,

in space."

The lady loutes adoun

And comlyly kysses his face;

Much speche thay ther expoun

Of druryes greme and grace.

"I woled wyt at yow, wyye," that worthy ther sayde,

"And yow wrathed not therwyth, what were the skylle

1510 That so yong and so yepe as ye at this tyme,

So cortayse, so knyghtyly, as ye ar knowen oute—

And of alle chevalry to chose, the chef thyng alosed

Is the lel layk of luf, the lettrure of armes;

For to telle of this tevelyng of this trwe knyghtes,

Hit is the tytelet token and tyxt of her werkkes,

How ledes for her lele luf hor lyves han auntered,

Endured for her drury dulful stoundes,

And after wenged with her walour and voyded her care,

though if discourtesy has occurred then correct me, of course."
"I encouraged you to kiss," the lady said kindly,
1490 "and to claim one quickly when one is required,
an act which ennobles any knight worth the name."
"Dear lady," said the other, "don't think such a thing,
I dare not kiss in case I am declined.
If refused, I'd be at fault for offering in the first place."
"In truth," she told him, "you cannot be turned down.
If someone were so snooty as to snub your advance,
a man like you has the means of his muscles."
"Yes, by God," said Gawain, "what you say holds good.
But such heavy-handedness is frowned on in my homeland,
1500 and so is any gift not given with grace.
What kiss you request I will courteously supply,
have what you want or hold off, whichever
                        the case."
                So bending from above
                the fair one kissed his face.
                The two then talk of love:
                its grief; also its grace.

"I would like to learn," said the noble lady,
"and please find no offence, but how can it follow
1510 that a lord so lively and young in years,
a champion in chivalry across the country—
and in chivalry, the chiefmost aspect to choose,
as all knights acknowledge, is loyalty in love,
for when tales of truthful knights are told
in both title and text the topic they describe
is how lords have laid down their lives for love,
endured for many days love's dreadful ordeal,
then vented their feelings with avenging valor

And broght blysse into boure with bountees hor awen—
1520 And ye ar knyght comlokest kyd of your elde,
Your worde and your worchip walkes ayquere,
And I haf seten by yourself here sere twyes,
Yet herde I never of your hed helde no wordes
That ever longed to luf, lasse ne more.
And ye, that ar so cortays and coynt of your hetes,
Oghe to a yonke thynk yern to schewe
And teche sum tokenes of trweluf craftes.
Why! ar ye lewed, that alle the los weldes,
Other elles ye demen me to dille your dalyaunce to herken?
1530   For schame!
      I com hider sengel and sitte
      To lerne at yow sum game;
      Dos teches me of your wytte,
      Whil my lorde is fro hame."

"In goud faythe," quoth Gawayn, "God yow foryelde!
Gret is the gode gle, and gomen to me huge,
That so worthy as ye wolde wynne hidere,
And pyne yow with so pouer a mon, as play wyth your knyght
With anyskynnes countenaunce—hit keveres me ese.
1540 Bot to take the torvayle to myself to trwluf expoun,
And towche the temes of tyxt and tales of armes
To yow that, I wot wel, weldes more slyght
Of that art, bi the half, or a hundreth of seche
As I am other ever schal, in erde ther I leve—
Hit were a folé felefolde, my fre, by my trawthe.
I wolde yowre wylnyng worche at my myght,
As I am hyghly bihalden, and evermore wylle
Be servaunt to yourselven, so save me dryghtyn!"
Thus hym frayned that fre and fondet hym ofte,

by bringing great bliss to a lady's bedroom—

1520 and you the most notable of all noble knights,

whose fame goes before him . . . yes, how can it follow

that twice I have taken this seat at your side

yet you have not spoken the smallest syllable

which belongs to love or anything like it.

A knight so courteous and considerate in his service

really ought to be eager to offer this pupil

some lessons in love, and to lead by example.

Is he actually ignorant, this man of eminence,

or does he deem me too duncelike to hear of dalliances?

1530   I come

to learn of love and more,

a lady all alone.

Perform for me before

my husband heads for home."

"In faith," said Gawain, "may God grant you fortune.

It gives me great gladness and seems a good game

that a woman so worthy should want to come here

and be happy and good hearted with a humble knight

unfit for her favors—I am flattered indeed.

1540 But to take on the task of explaining true love

or touch on the topics those love tales tell of,

with yourself, who I sense has more insight and skill

in the art than I have, or even a hundred

of the likes of me, however long we live,

would be somewhat presumptuous, I have to say.

But to the best of my ability I'll do your bidding,

bound as I am to honor you forever

and to serve you as long as our Savior preserves me!"

So the lady tempted and teased him, trying

For to haf wonnen hym to woghe, what-so scho thoght elles;
Bot he defended hym so fayr that no faut semed,
Ne non evel on nawther halve, nawther thay wysten
                    bot blysse.
              Thay laghed and layked longe;
              At the last scho con hym kysse,
              Hir leve fayre con scho fonge,
              And went hir waye, iwysse.

Then ruthes hym the renk and ryses to the masse,
And sithen hor diner was dyght and derely served.
The lede with the ladyes layked alle day,
Bot the lorde over the londes launced ful ofte,
Swes his uncely swyn, that swynges bi the bonkkes
And bote the best of his braches the bakkes in sunder
Ther he bode in his bay, tel bawemen hit breken,
And madee hym, mawgref his hed, for to mwe utter,
So felle flones ther flete when the folk gedered.
Bot yet the styffest to start bi stoundes he made,
Til at the last he was so mat he myght no more renne,
Bot in the hast that he myght he to a hole wynnes
Of a rasse, bi a rokk ther rennes the boerne.
He gete the bonk at his bak, bigynes to scrape,
The frothe femed at his mouth unfayre bi the wykes,
Whettes his whyte tusches. With hym then irked
Alle the burnes so bolde that hym by stoden
To nye hym on-ferum, bot neghe hym non durst
                    for wothe.
              He hade hurt so mony byforne
              That al thught thenne ful lothe
              Be more wyth his tusches torne,
              That breme was and braynwod bothe.

1550 to enmesh him in whatever mischief she had in mind.
But fairly and without fault he defended himself,
no evil in either of them, only ecstasy
                    that day.
                    At length, when they had laughed,
                    the woman kissed Gawain.
                    Politely then she left
                    and went her own sweet way.

Roused and risen he was ready for mass.
The meal of the morning was made and served,
1560 then he loitered with the ladies the length of the day
while the lord of the land ranged left and right
in pursuit of that pig which stampeded through the uplands,
breaking his best hounds with its back-snapping bite
when it stood embattled . . . then bowmen would strike,
goading it to gallop into open ground
where the air was alive with the huntsman's arrows.
That boar made the best men flinch and bolt,
till at last his legs were like lead beneath him,
and he hobbled away to hunker in a hole
1570 by a stony rise at the side of a stream.
With the bank at his back he scrapes and burrows,
frothing and foaming foully at the mouth,
whetting his white tusks. The hunters waited,
irked by the effort of aiming from afar
but daunted by the danger of daring to venture
                    too near.
                    So many men before
                    had fallen prey. They feared
                    that fierce and frenzied boar
1580   whose tusks could slash and tear.

Til the knyght com hymself, kachande his blonk,
Syy hym byde at the bay, his burnes bysyde.
He lyghtes luflych adoun, leves his corsour,
Braydes out a bryght bront and bigly forth strydes,
Foundes fast thurgh the forth ther the felle bydes.
The wylde was war of the wyye with weppen in honde,
Hef hyghly the here, so hetterly he fnast
That fele ferde for the freke, lest felle hym the worre.
The swyn settes hym out on the segge even,
1590   That the burne and the bor were bothe upon hepes
In the wyghtest of the water. The worre hade that other,
For the mon merkkes hym wel, as thay mette fyrst,
Set sadly the scharp in the slot even,
Hit hym up to the hult, that the hert schyndered,
And he yarrande hym yelde, and yedoun the water
                    ful tyt.
            A hundreth houndes hym hent,
            That bremely con hym bite;
            Burnes him broght to bent
1600   And dogges to dethe endite.

There was blawyng of prys in mony breme horne,
Heghe halowing on highe with hatheles that myght;
Brachetes bayed that best, as bidden the maysteres,
Of that chargeaunt chace that were chef huntes.
Thenne a wyye that was wys upon wodcraftes
To unlace this bor lufly bigynnes:
Fyrst he hewes of his hed and on highe settes,
And sythen rendes him al roghe bi the rygge after,
Braydes out the boweles, brennes hom on glede,
1610   With bred blent therwith his braches rewardes.
Sythen he britnes out the brawen in bryght brode scheldes,

Till his lordship hacks up, urging on his horse,
spots the swine at standstill encircled by men,
then handsomely dismounts and unhands his horse,
brandishes a bright sword and goes bounding onwards,
wades through the water to where the beast waits.
Aware that the man was wafting a weapon
the hog's hairs stood on end, and its howling grunt
made the fellows there fear for their master's fate.
Then the boar burst forward, bounded at the lord,
1590 so that beast and hunter both went bundling
into white water, and the swine came off worst,
because the moment they clashed the man found his mark,
knifing the boar's neck, nailing his prey,
hammering it to the hilt, bursting the hog's heart.
Screaming, it was swept downstream, almost slipping
               beneath.
          At least a hundred hounds
          latch on with tearing teeth.
          Then, dragged to drier ground,
1600   the dogs complete its death.

The kill was blown on many blaring bugle
and the unhurt hunters hollered and whooped.
The chief amongst them, in charge of the chase,
commanded the bloodhounds to bay at the boar,
then one who was wise in woodland ways
began carefully to cut and carve up the carcass.
First he hacks off its head and hoists it aloft,
then roughly rives it right along the spine;
he gouges out the guts and grills them over coals,
1610 and blended with bread they are tidbits for the bloodhounds.
Next he fetches out the fillets of glimmering flesh

And has out the hastlettes, as hightly bisemes;
And yet hem halches al hole the halves togeder,
And sythen on a stif stange stoutly hem henges.
Now with this ilk swyn thay swengen to home;
The bores hed was borne bifore the burnes selven,
That him forferde in the forthe thurgh forse of his honde
        so stronge.
      Til he sey Sir Gawayne
1620   In halle hym thoght ful longe;
      He calde, and he com gayn
      His fees ther for to fonge.

The lorde, ful lowde with lote, laghed myry
When he seye Sir Gawayn; with solace he spekes.
The goude ladyes were geten, and gedered the meyny;
He schewes hem the scheldes and schapes hem the tale
Of the largesse and the lenthe, the lithernes also,
Of the were of the wylde swyn in wod ther he fled.
That other knyght ful comly comended his dedes,
1630 And praysed hit as gret prys that he proved hade;
For suche a brawne of a best, the bolde burne sayde,
Ne such sydes of a swyn segh he never are.
Thenne hondeled thay the hoge hed, the hende mon hit praysed,
And let lodly therat the lorde for to here.
"Now, Gawayn," quoth the godmon, "this gomen is your awen
Bi fyn forwarde and faste, faythely ye knowe."
"Hit is sothe," quoth the segge, "and as siker trwe
Alle my get I schal yow gif agayn, bi my trawthe."
He hent the hathel aboute the halse and hendely hym kysses,
1640 And eftersones of the same he served hym there.
"Now ar we even," quoth the hathel, "in this eventide,

and retrieves the intestines in time-honored style,
then the two sides are stitched together intact
and proudly displayed on a strong pole.
So with the swine swinging they swagger home,
bearing the boar's head before that huntsman
who had fought with his fists in the ford till the beast
was slain.
The day then dragged, it seemed,
1620   before he found Gawain,
who comes when called, most keen
to countenance the claim.

Now the lord is loud with words and laughter
and speaks excitedly when he sees Sir Gawain;
he calls for the ladies plus the company of the court
and he shows off the meat slabs and shares the story
of the hog's hulking hugeness, and the full horror
of the fight to the finish as it fled through the forest.
And Gawain is quick to compliment the conquest,
1630 praising it as proof of the lord's prowess,
for such prime pieces of perfect pork
and such sides of swine were a sight to be seen.
Then admiringly he handles the hog's great head,
feigning fear to flatter the master's feelings.
"Now Gawain," said the lord, "I give you this game,
as our wager warranted, as well you remember."
"Certainly," said Sir Gawain. "It shall be so.
And graciously I shall give you my gains in exchange."
He catches him by the neck and courteously kisses him,
1640 then a second time kisses him in a similar style.
"Now we're even," said Gawain, "at this evening's end;

Of alle the covenauntes that we knyt, sythen I com hider,
       bi lawe."
      The lorde sayde: "Bi saynt Gile,
      Ye ar the best that I knawe;
      Ye ben ryche in a whyle,
      Such chaffer and ye drawe."

Thenne thay teldet tables trestes alofte,
Kesten clothes upon. Clere lyght thenne
1650 Wakned bi wowes, waxen torches
Segges sette, and served in sale al aboute.
Much glam and gle glent up therinne
Aboute the fyre upon flet, and on fele wyse
At the soper and after, mony athel songes,
As coundutes of Krystmasse and caroles newe,
With alle the manerly merthe that mon may of telle,
And ever oure luflych knyght the lady bisyde.
Such semblaunt to that segge semly ho made,
Wyth stille stollen countenaunce, that stalworth to plese,
1660 That al forwondered was the wyye, and wroth with hymselven;
Bot he nolde not for his nurture nurne hir ayaynes,
Bot dalt with hir al in daynté, how-se-ever the dede turned
       towrast.
      Quen thay hade played in halle
      As longe as hor wylle hom last,
      To chambre he con hym calle,
      And to the chemné thay past.

Ande ther thay dronken and dalten, and demed eft nwe
To norne on the same note on Nwe Yeres even;
1670 Bot the knyght craved leve to kayre on the morn,
For hit was negh at the terme that he to schulde.

the clauses of our contract have been kept and you have what
     I owe."
     "By Saint Giles," the just lord says,
     "This knight's the best I know.
     By wagering this way
     his gains will grow and grow."

Then the trestle tables were swiftly assembled
and cast with fine cloths. A clear, living light
1650 from the waxen torches awakened the walls.
Places were set and supper was served,
and a din arose as they reveled in a ring
around the fire in the fireplace, and the feasting party
sang song after song, at supper and beyond,
both traditional ditties and carols of the day,
with as much amusement as a mouth could mention.
The young woman and Gawain sat together all the while.
And so loving was that lady towards the young lord,
with stolen glances and secret smiles
1660 that it muddled his mind and sent him half mad,
but to snub a noblewoman was not in his nature,
and though tongues might wag he returned her attention
     all night.
     Before his friends retire
     his lordship leads the knight,
     heads for his hearth and fire
     to linger by its light.

They supped and swapped stories, and spoke again
of the night to come next, which was New Year's Eve.
1670 Gawain pleaded politely to depart by morning,
so in two days' time he might honor his treaty.

The lorde hym letted of that, to lenge hym resteyed,
And sayde: "As I am trwe segge, I siker my trawthe
Thou schal cheve to the grene chapel, thy charres to make,
Leude, on Nw Yeres lyght, longe bifore pryme.
Forthy thow lye in thy loft and lach thyn ese,
And I schal hunt in this holt and halde the towches,
Chaunge wyth the chevisaunce, bi that I charre hider;
For I haf fraysted the twys, and faythful I fynde the.
1680   Now "thrid tyme, throwe best," thenk on the morne;
Make we mery quyl we may, and mynne upon joye,
For the lur may mon lach when-so mon lykes."
This was graythely graunted, and Gawayn is lenged;
Blithe broght was hym drynk, and thay to bedde yeden

>with light.
>   Sir Gawayn lis and slepes
>   Ful stille and softe al night;
>   The lorde that his craftes kepes,
>   Ful erly he was dight.

1690   After messe a morsel he and his men token;
Miry was the mornyng, his mounture he askes.
Alle the hatheles that on horse schulde helden hym after
Were boun busked on hor blonkkes bifore the halle yates.
Ferly fayre was the folde, for the forst clenged,
In rede rudede upon rak rises the sunne,
And ful clere castes the clowdes of the welkyn.
Hunteres unhardeled bi a holt syde,
Rocheres roungen bi rys for rurde of her hornes.
Summe fel in the fute ther the fox bade,
1700   Trayles ofte a traveres bi traunt of her wyles.
A kenet kryes therof, the hunt on hym calles;
His felawes fallen hym to, that fnasted ful thike,

But the lord was unswerving, insisting that he stayed:
"As an honest soul I swear on my heart,
you shall find the Green Chapel to finalize your affairs
long before dawn on New Year's Day.
So lie in your room and laze at your leisure
while I ride my estate, and, as our terms dictate,
we'll trade our trophies when the hunt returns.
I have tested you twice and found you truthful.
But think tomorrow *third time throw best.*
Now, a lord can feel low whenever he likes,
so let's chase cheerfulness while we have the chance."
So those gentlemen agreed that Gawain would stay,
and they took more drink, then by torchlight retired to
                    their beds.
              Our man then sleeps, a most
              reposed and peaceful rest.
              As hunters must, his host
              is up at dawn and dressed.

After mass the master grabs a meal with his men
and asks for his mount on that marvelous morning.
All those grooms engaged to go with their lord
were high on their horses before the hall gates.
The fields were dazzling, fixed with frost,
and the crown of sunrise rose scarlet and crimson,
scalding and scattering cloud from the sky.
At the fringe of the forest the dogs were set free
and the rumpus of the horns went ringing through the rocks.
They fall on the scent of a fox, and follow,
turning and twisting as they sniff out the trail.
A young harrier yowls and a huntsman yells,
then the pack come rushing to pick up the reek,

Runnen forth in a rabel in his ryght fare.

And he fyskes hem byfore; thay founden hym sone,

And quen thay seghe hym with syght thay sued hym fast,

Wreyande hym ful weterly with a wroth noyse;

And he trantes and tornayees thurgh mony tene greve,

Havilounes and herkenes bi hegges ful ofte.

At the last bi a littel dich he lepes over a spenné

1710 Steles out ful stilly bi a strothe rande,

Went haf wylt of the wode with wyles fro the houndes.

Thenne was he went, er he wyst, to a wale tryster,

Ther thre thro at a thrich thrat hym at ones,

al graye.

He blenched ayayn bilyve

And stifly start onstray;

With alle the wo on lyve

To the wod he went away.

Thenne was hit list upon lif to lythen the houndes,

1720 When alle the mute hade hym met, menged togeder.

Suche a sorwe at that syght thay sette on his hede

As alle the clamberande clyffes hade clatered on hepes.

Here he was halawed when hatheles hym metten,

Loude he was yayned with yarande speche;

Ther he was threted and ofte thef called,

And ay the titleres at his tayl, that tary he ne myght,

Ofte he was runnen at when he out rayked,

And ofte reled in ayayn, so Reniarde was wylé.

And ye he lad hem bi lag-mon, the lorde and his meyny,

1730 On this maner bi the mountes quyle myd-over-under,

Whyle the hende knyght at home holsumly slepes

Withinne the comly cortynes, on the colde morne.

Bot the lady for luf let not to slepe,

running as a rabble along the right track.

The fox scurries ahead, they scamper behind,

and pursue him at speed when he comes within sight,

haranguing him with horrific ranting howls.

Now and then he doubles back through thorny thickets,

or halts and harkens in the hem of a hedge,

until finally, by a hollow, he hurdles a fence,

1710 and carefully he creeps by the edge of a copse,

convinced that his cunning has conned those canines!

But unawares he wanders where they lie in wait,

where greyhounds are gathered together, a group

                of three.

        He springs back with a start,

        then twists and turns and flees.

        With heavy, heaving heart

        he tracks towards the trees.

Such earthly elation, hearing those hounds

1720 as they massed to meet him, marauding together,

and they bayed bloodily at the sight of his being,

as if clustering cliffs had crashed to the ground.

Here he was ambushed by bushwhacking huntsmen

waiting with a welcome of wounding words;

there he was threatened and branded a thief,

and always the hounds allowed him no ease.

Often, in the open, the pack tried to pounce,

then that crafty Reynard would creep into cover.

So his lordship and his lords were merrily led

1730 in this manner through the mountains until midafternoon,

while our handsome hero snoozed contentedly at home,

kept from the cold of the morning by curtains.

But love would not let her ladyship sleep

Ne the purpose to payre, that pyght in hir hert,

Bot ros hir up radly, rayked hir theder

In a mery mantyle, mete to the erthe,

That was furred ful fyne with felles wel pured;

No hwe goud on hir hede, bot the hagher stones

Trased aboute hir tressour be twenty in clusteres;

1740 Hir thryven face and hir throte throwen al naked,

Hir brest bare bifore, and bihinde eke.

Ho comes withinne the chambre dore and closes hit hir after,

Wayves up a wyndow and on the wyye calles,

And radly thus rehayted hym with hir riche wordes,

    with chere:

  "A! mon, how may thou slepe?

  This morning is so clere."

  He was in drowping depe,

  Bot thenne he con hir here.

1750 In drey droupying of dreme draveled that noble,

As mon that was in mornyng of mony thro thoghtes,

How that destiné schulde that day dele hym his wyrde

At the grene chapel, when he the gome metes,

And bihoves his buffet abide withoute debate more.

Bot quen that comly he kevered his wyttes,

Swenges out of the swevenes and swares with hast.

The lady luflych com laghande swete,

Felle over his fayre face and fetly hym kyssed.

He welcumes hir worthily with a wale chere;

1760 He sey hir so glorious and gayly atyred,

So fautles of hir fetures and of so fyne hewes,

Wight wallande joye warmed his hert.

With smothe smylyng and smolt thay smeten into merthe,

and the fervor she felt in her heart would not fade.
She rose from her rest and rushed to his room
in a flowing robe that reached to the floor
and was finished inside with fine-trimmed furs.
Her head went unhooded, but heavenly gems
were entwined in her tresses in clusters of twenty.

1740 She wore nothing on her face; her neck was naked,
and her shoulders were bare to both back and breast.
She comes into his quarters and closes the door,
makes her way to the window and throws it open,
then sweet and swift is the speech she intends for
                  his ear.
          "Oh, sir, how can you sleep
          when morning comes so clear?"
          And though his dreams are deep
          he cannot help but hear.

1750 Yes he dozes in a daze, dreams and mutters
like a mournful man with his mind on dark matters—
how destiny might deal him a death blow on the day
when he grapples with the giant in the Green Chapel;
of how the strike of the axe must be suffered without struggle.
But sensing her presence there he surfaces from sleep,
drags himself out of his dreams to address her.
Laughing warmly she walks towards him
and finds his face with the friendliest kiss.
In a worthy style he welcomes the woman

1760 and seeing her so lovely and alluringly dressed,
every feature so faultless, her complexion so fine,
a passionate heat takes hold in his heart.
Speech tripped from their tongues and they traded smiles,

That al was blis and bonchef that breke hem bitwene,

and wynne.

Thay lauced wordes gode,

Much wele then was therinne;

Gret perile bitwene hem stod,

Nif Maré of hir knyght con mynne.

1770 For that prynces of pris depresed hym so thikke,

Nurned hym so neghe the thred, that nede hym bihoved

Other lach ther hir luf other lodly refuse.

He cared for his cortaysye, lest crathayn he were,

And more for his meschef, yif he schulde make synne

And be traytor to that tolke that that telde aght.

"God schylde," quoth the schalk, "that schal not befalle!"

With luf-laghyng a lyt he layd hym bysyde

Alle the speches of specialté that sprange of her mouthe.

Quoth that burde to the burne: "Blame ye disserve,

1780 Yif ye luf not that lyf that ye lye nexte,

Bifore alle the wyyes in the worlde wounded in hert,

Bot if ye haf a lemman, a lever, that yow lykes better,

And folden fayth to that fre, festned so harde

That yow lausen ne lyst—and that I leve nouthe.

And that ye telle me that now trwly, I pray yow;

For alle the lufes upon lyve, layne not the sothe

for gile."

The knyght sayde: "Be sayn Jon,"

And smethely con he smyle,

1790 "In fayth I welde right non,

Ne non wil welde the quile."

"That is a worde," quoth that wyght, "that worst is of alle;

Bot I am swared for sothe, that sore me thinkkes.

and a bond of friendship was forged there, all blissful
                    and bright.
             They talk with tenderness
             and pride, and yet their plight
             is perilous unless
             sweet Mary minds her knight.

1770   For that noble princess pushed him and pressed him,
       nudged him ever nearer to a limit where he needed
       to allow her love or impolitely reject it.
       He was careful to be courteous and avoid uncouthness,
       cautious that his conduct might be classed as sinful
       and counted as betrayal by the keeper of the castle.
       "I shall not succumb," he swore to himself.
       With affectionate laughter he fenced and deflected
       all the loving phrases which leapt from her lips.
       "You shall bear the blame," said the beautiful one,
1780   "if you feel no love for the female you lie with,
       and wound her, more than anyone on earth, to the heart.
       Unless, of course, there is a lady in your life
       to whom you are tied and so tightly attached
       that you could not begin to break the bond.
       So in honesty and trust now tell me the truth;
       for the sake of all love, don't be secretive or speak
                    with guile."
             "You judge wrong, by Saint John,"
             he said to her, and smiled.
1790   "There is no other one
             and won't be for a while!"

"Those words," said the woman, "are the worst insult.
But I asked, and you answered, and now I ache.

Kysse me now comly, and I schal cach hethen;

I may bot mourne upon molde, as may that much lovyes."

Sykande ho sweye doun and semly hym kyssed,

And sithen ho severes hym fro, and says as ho stondes:

"Now, dere, at this departyng, do me this ese,

Gif me sumquat of thy gifte, thi glove if hit were,

1800   That I may mynne on the, mon, my mournyng to lassen."

"Now iwysse," quoth that wyye, "I wolde I hade here

The levest thing for thy luf that I in londe welde,

For ye haf deserved, for sothe, sellyly ofte

More rewarde bi resoun then I reche myght;

Bot to dele yow for drurye, that dawed bot neked.

Hit is not your honour to haf at this tyme

A glove for a garysoun of Gawaynes giftes;

And I am here on an erande in erdes uncouthe,

And have no men wyth no males with menskful thinges.

1810   That mislykes me, ladé, for thy luf at this tyme;

Iche tolke mon do as he is tan, tas to non ille

ne pine."

"Nay, hende of hyghe honours,"

Quoth that lufsum under lyne,

"Thagh I hade noght of youres,

Yet schulde ye have of myne."

Ho raght hym a riche rynk of red golde werkes,

Wyth a starande ston stondande alofte,

That bere blusschande bemes as the bryght sunne;

1820   Wyt ye wel, hit was worth wele ful hoge.

Bot the renk hit renayed, and redyly he sayde:

"I wil no giftes for Gode, my gay, at this tyme;

I haf none yow to norne, ne noght wyl I take."

Ho bede hit hym ful bysily, and he hir bode wernes,

Kiss me warmly and then I will walk in the world
in mourning like a lady who loved too much."
Stooping and sighing she kisses him sweetly,
then withdraws from his side, saying as she stands,
"But before we part will you find me some small favor?
Will you give me some gift—a glove at least,
1800 that might leaven my loss when we meet in my memory."
"Well it were," said Gawain. "I wish I had here
my most priceless possession as a present for your sweetness,
for over and over you deserve and are owed
the highest prize I could hope to offer.
But I would not wish on you a worthless token,
and it strikes me as unseemly that you should receive
nothing greater than a glove as a keepsake from Gawain.
I am here on an errand in an unknown land
without men bearing bags of beautiful gifts,
1810 which I greatly regret through my regard for you;
but man must live by his means, and neither mope
            or moan."
        The pretty one replies:
        "Nay, noble knight, you mean
        you'll pass to me no prize.
        No matter. Here is mine."

She offers him a ring of rich, red gold,
and the stunning stone set upon it stood proud,
beaming and burning with the brightness of the sun;
1820 what wealth it was worth you can well imagine.
But he would not accept it, and said straight away,
"By God, no tokens will I take at this time;
I have nothing to give, so nothing will I gain."
She insists he receives it but still he resists,

And swere swyftely his sothe that he hit sese nolde;

And ho sore that he forsoke, and sayde therafter:

"If ye renay my rynk, to ryche for hit semes,

Ye wolde not so hyghly halden be to me,

I schal gif yow my girdel, that gaynes yow lasse."

1830 Ho laght a lace lyghtly that leke umbe hir sydes,

Knit upon hir kyrtel under the clere mantyle.

Gered hit was with grene sylke and with golde schaped,

Noght bot aronde brayden, beten with fyngres;

And that ho bede to the burne, and blythely bisoght,

Thagh hit unworthi were, that he hit take wolde.

And he nay that he nolde neghe in no wyse

Nauther golde ne garysoun, er God hym grace sende

To acheve to the chaunce that he hade chosen there.

"And therfore, I pray yow, displese yow noght,

1840 And lettes be your bisinesse, for I baythe hit yow never

to graunte.

I am derely to yow biholde

Bicause of your sembelaunt,

And ever in hot and colde

To be your trwe servaunt."

"Now forsake ye this silke," sayde the burde thenne,

"For hit is symple in hitself? And so hit wel semes.

Lo! so hit is littel, and lasse hit is worthy.

Bot who-so knew the costes that knit ar therinne.

1850 He wolde hit prayse at more prys, paraventure;

For quat gome so is gorde with this grene lace,

While he hit hade hemely halched aboute,

Ther is no hathel under heven tohewe hym that myght,

For he myght not be slayn for slyght upon erthe."

Then kest the knyght, and hit come to his hert,

and swears, on his name as a knight, to say no.
Snubbed by his decision, she said to him then,
"You refuse my ring because you find it too fine,
and don't dare to be deeply indebted to me;
so I give you my girdle, a lesser thing to gain."
1830 From around her body she unbuckled the belt
which tightened the tunic beneath her topcoat,
a green silk girdle trimmed with gold,
exquisitely edged and hemmed by hand.
And she sweetly beseeched Sir Gawain to receive it,
in spite of its slightness, and hoped he would accept.
But still he maintained he intended to take
neither gold nor girdle, until by God's grace
the challenge he had chosen was finally achieved.
"With apologies I pray you are not displeased,
1840 but I must firmly refuse you, no matter how flattered
                    I am.
            For all your grace I owe
            a thousand thank-you's, ma'am.
            I shall through sun and snow
            remain your loyal man."

"And now he sends back my silk," the lady responded,
"so simple in itself, or so it appears,
so little and unlikely, worth nothing, or less.
But the knight who knew of the power knitted in it
1850 would pay a high price to possess it, probably.
For the body which is bound within this green belt,
as long as it is buckled robustly about him,
will be safe against those who seek to strike him,
and all the slyness on earth wouldn't see him slain."
The man mulled it over, and it entered his mind

Hit were a juel for the jopardé that hym jugged were,
When he acheved to the chapel, his chek for to fech;
Myght he haf slypped to be unslayn, the sleght were noble.
Thenne he thulged with hir threpe and tholed hir to speke.
1860 And ho bere on hym the belt and bede hit hym swythe;
And he granted, and ho hym gafe with a goud wylle,
And bisoght hym, for hir sake, discever hit never,
Bot to lelly layne fro hir lorde. The leude hym acordes
That never wyye schulde hit wyt, iwysse, bot thay twayne,
        for noghte.
            He thonkked hir oft ful swythe,
            Ful thro with hert and thoght.
            Bi that on thrynne sythe
            Ho has kyst the knyght so toght.

1870 Thenne lachches ho hir leve and leves hym there,
For more myrthe of that mon moght ho not gete.
When ho was gon, Sir Gawayn geres hym sone,
Rises and riches hym in araye noble,
Lays up the luf-lace the lady hym raght,
Hid hit ful holdely ther he hit eft fonde.
Sythen chevely to the chapel choses he the waye,
Prevely aprched to a prest, and prayed hym there
That he wolde lyfte his lyf and lern hym better
How his sawle schulde be saved when he schuld seye hethen.
1880 There he schrof hym schyrly and schewed his mysdedes
Of the more and the mynne, and merci beseches,
And of absolucioun he on the segge calles;
And he asoyled hym surely and sette hym so clene
As domesday schulde haf ben dight on the morn.
And sythen he mace hym as mery among the fre ladyes,
With comlych caroles and alle kynnes joye,

that this girdle being given could be just the job
to save him from the strike in his challenge at the chapel.
With luck, it might let him escape with his life.
So relenting at last he let her speak,

1860   and promptly she pressed him to take the present,
and he granted her wish, gave in with good grace,
though the woman begged him not to whisper a word
of this gift to her husband, and Gawain agreed;
those words of theirs within those walls
                         should stay.
              His thanks are heartfelt, then.
              No sooner can he say
              how much it matters, when
              three kisses come his way.

1870   Then the lady departed, leaving him alone,
for the man had amused her as much as he could.
And once she has quit he clothes himself quickly,
rises and dresses in the richest of robes,
stowing the love-lace safely aside,
hiding it away from all hands and eyes.
Then he went at once to the chapel of worship,
privately approached the priest and implored him
to allow his confession, and to lead him in life
so his soul might be saved when he goes to his grave.

1880   Then fully and frankly he spoke of his sins,
no matter how small, always seeking mercy,
calling on that counselor to clear his conscience.
The priest declares him so clean and so pure
that the Day of Doom could dawn in the morning.
Then in merrier mood he mingled with the ladies,
caroling and carousing and carrying on

As never he did bot that daye, to the derk nyght,
              with blys.
          Uche mon hade daynté thare
1890   Of hym, and sayde: "Iwysse,
          Thus myry he was never are,
          Syn he com hider, er this."

Now hym lenge in that lee, ther luf hym bityde!
Yet is the lorde on the launde, ledande his gomnes.
He has forfaren this fox that he folwed longe.
As he sprent over a spenné to spye the schrewe,
Ther as he herd the howndes that hasted hym swythe,
Renaud com richchande thurgh a roghe greve,
And alle the rabel in a res, ryght at his heles.
1900 The wyye was war of the wylde and warly abides,
And braydes out the bryght bronde and at the best castes.
And he schunt for the scharp and schulde haf arered;
A rach rapes hym to, ryght er he myght,
And ryght bifore the hors fete thay fel on hym alle
And woried me this wyly wyth a wroth noyse.
The lorde lyghtes bilyve and laches hym sone,
Rased hym ful radly out of the rach mouthes,
Haldes heghe over his hede, halowes faste,
And ther bayen hym mony brath houndes.
1910 Huntes hyyed hem theder with hornes ful mony,
Ay rechatande aryght til thay the renk seyen.
Bi that was comen his compeyny noble,
Alle that ever ber bugle blowed at ones,
And alle thise other halowed, that hade no hornes.
Hit was the myriest mute that ever men herde,
The rich rurd that ther was raysed for Renaude saule
              with lote.

as never before, until nightfall. Folk feel
>
> and hear
>
> and see his boundless bliss
>
> 1890 and say, "Such charm and cheer;
>
> he's at his happiest
>
> since his arrival here."

And long let him loiter there, looked after by love.
Now the lord of the land was still leading his men,
finishing off the fox he had followed for so long.
He vaults a fence to flush out the victim,
hearing that the hounds are harrying hard.
Then Reynard scoots from a section of scrub
and the rabble of the pack rush right at his heels.
1900 Aware of its presence the wary lord waits,
then bares his bright sword and swishes at the beast,
which shirks from its sharpness, and would have shot away
but a hound flew forward before it could flee
and under the hooves of the horses they have him,
worrying their quarry with woeful wailing.
The lord hurtles from his horse and heaves the fox up,
wrestles it from the reach of those ravenous mouths,
holds it high over head and hurrahs manfully
while the bloodthirsty bloodhounds bay and howl.
1910 And the other huntsmen hurried with their horns
to catch sight of the slaughter and celebrate the kill.
And when the company of clansmen had come together
the buglers blew with one mighty blast,
and the others hallooed with open throats.
A human could not hear a headier music
than the rapturous roar which for Reynard's soul

> was raised.

Hor houndes thay ther rewarde,
Her hedes thay fawne and frote;
1920   And sythen thay tan Reynarde
And tyrven of his cote.

And thenne thay helden to home, for hit was niegh nyght,
Strakande ful stoutly in hor store hornes.
The lorde is lyght at the laste at hys lef home,
Fyndes fire upon flet, the freke ther-byside,
Sir Gawayn the gode that glad was withalle—
Among the ladies for luf he ladde much joye.
He were a bleaunt of blwe that bradde to the erthe.
His surkot semed hym wel that softe was forred,
1930 And his hode of that ilke henged on his schulder,
Blande al of blaunner were bothe al aboute.
He metes me this godmon inmyddes the flore,
And al with gomen he hym gret, and goudly he sayde:
"I schal fylle upon fyrst oure forwardes nouthe,
That we spedly han spoken ther spared was no drynk."
Then acoles he the knyght and kysses hym thryes,
As saverly and sadly as he hem sette couthe.
"Bi Kryst," quoth that other knyght, "ye cach much sele
In chevisaunce of this chaffer, yif ye hade goud chepes."
1940 "Ye, of the chepe no charg," quoth chefly that other,
"As is pertly payed the chepes that I aghte."
"Mary," quoth that other mon, "myn is bihynde,
For I haf hunted al this day, and noght haf I geten
Bot this foule fox felle—the fende haf the godes!—
And that is ful pore for to pay for suche prys thinges
As ye haf thryght me here thro, suche thre cosses
                    so gode."

The dogs, due their reward,
are patted, stroked and praised.
1920   Then red fur rips—Reynard
out of his pelt is prized.

Then with night drawing near they headed homewards,
blaring their bugles with the fullness of their breath.
And at last the lord lands at his lovely home,
to find, by the heat of the fireside, his friend
the good Sir Gawain, in glad spirits
on account of the company he had kept with the ladies.
His blue robe flowed as far as the floor,
his soft-furred surcoat suited him well,
1930   and the hood which echoed it hung from his shoulders.
Both hood and coat were edged in ermine.
He meets the master in the middle of the room,
greets him graciously, with Gawain saying:
"I shall first fulfil our formal agreement
which we fixed in words when the drink flowed freely."
He clasps him tight and kisses him three times
with as much emotion as a man could muster.
"By the Almighty," said the master, "you must have had luck
to profit such a prize—if the price was right."
1940   "Oh fiddlesticks to the fee," said the other fellow.
"As long as I have given the goods which I gained."
"By Mary," said the master, "mine's a miserable match.
I've hunted for hours with nothing to my name
but this foul-stinking fox—fling its fur to the devil—
so poor in comparison with your priceless prizes,
these presents you impart, three kisses perfect
                    and true."

"Inogh," quoth Sir Gawayn,
"I thonk yow, bi the rode."
1950 And how the fox was slayn
He tolde hym as thay stode.

With merthe and mynstralsye, wyth metes at hor wylle,
Thay maden as mery as any men moghten,
With laghyng of ladies, with lotes of bordes.
Gawayn and the godemon so glad were thay bothe,
Bot if the douthe had doted other dronken ben other.
Bothe the mon and the meyny maden mony japes,
Til the sesoun was seyen that thay sever moste;
Burnes to hor bedde behoved at the laste.
1960 Thenne lowly his leve at the lorde fyrst
Fochches this fre mon, and fayre he hym thonkkes:
"Of such a selly sojorne as I haf hade here,
Your honour at this hyghe fest, the hyghe kyng yow yelde!
I yef yow me for on of youres, if yowreself lykes;
For I mot nedes, as ye wot, meve to-morne,
And ye me take sum tolke to teche, as ye hyght,
The gate to the grene chapel, as God wyl me suffer
To dele on Nw Yeres day the dome of my wyrdes."
"In god faythe," quoth the godmon, "wyth a goud wylle
1970 Al that ever I yow hyght, halde schal I redé."
Ther asyngnes he a servaunt to sett hym in the waye
And coundue hym by the downes, that he no drechch had,
For to ferk thurgh the fryth and fare at the gaynest
bi greve.
The lorde Gawayn con thonk,
Such worchip he wolde hym weve.
Then at tho ladyes wlonk
The knyght has tan his leve.

"Enough!" the knight entreats,
"I thank you through and through."
1950 The standing lord then speaks
of how the fox fur flew!

And with meals and mirth and minstrelsy
they made as much amusement as any mortal could,
and among those merry men and laughing ladies
Gawain and his host got giddy together;
only lunatics and drunkards could have looked more delirious.
Every person present performed party pieces
till the hour arrived when revelers must rest,
and the company in that court heard the call of their beds.
1960 And lastly, in the hall, humbly to his host,
our knight says good night and renews his gratitude.
"Your uncountable courtesies have kept me here
this Christmas—be honored by the High King's kindness.
If it suits, I submit myself as your servant.
But tomorrow morning I must make a move;
if you will, as you promised, please appoint some person
to guide me, God willing, towards the Green Chapel,
where my destiny will dawn on New Year's Day."
"On my honor," he replied. "With hand on heart,
1970 every promise I made shall be put into practice."
He assigns him a servant to steer his course,
to lead him through the land without losing time,
to ride the fastest route between forest
                and fell.
        Gawain will warmly thank
        his host in terms that tell;
        towards the womenfolk
        the knight then waves farewell.

With care and wyth kyssyng he carppes hem tille,
1980 And fele thryvande thonkkes he thrat hom to have;
And thay yelden hym ayayn yeply that ilk.
Thay bikende hym to Kryst with ful colde sykynges.
Sythen fro the meyny he menskly departes;
Uche mon that he mette, he made hem a thonke
For his servyse and his solace and his sere pyne
That thay wyth busynes had ben aboute hym to serve;
And uche segge as sore to sever with hym there
As thay hade wonde worthyly with that wlonk ever.
Then with ledes and lyght he was ladde to his chambre,
1990 And blythely broght to his bedde to be at his rest.
Yif he ne slepe soundyly, say ne dar I,
For he hade muche on the morn to mynne, yif he wolde,
        in thoght.
      Let hym lyye there stille,
      He has nere that he soght;
      And ye wyl a whyle be stylle,
      I schal telle yow how thay wroght.

It's with a heavy heart that guests in the hall
1980 are kissed and thanked for their care and kindness,
and they respond with speeches of the same sort,
commending him to our Savior with sorrowful sighs.
Then politely he leaves the lord and his household,
and to each person he passes he imparts his thanks
for taking such trouble in their service and assistance
and such attention to detail in attendance of duty.
And every guest is grieved at the prospect of his going,
as if honorable Gawain were one of their own.
By tapering torchlight he was taken to his room
1990 and brought to his bed to be at his rest.
But if our knight sleeps soundly I couldn't say,
for the matter in the morning might be muddying
                his thoughts.
        So let him lie and think,
        in sight of what he sought.
        In time I'll tell if tricks
        work out the way they ought.

IV

Now neghes the Nw Yere and the nyght passes,
The day dryves to the derk, as dryghtyn biddes.
2000 Bot wylde wederes of the worlde wakned theroute,
Clowdes kesten kenly the colde to the erthe,
Wyth nyye innoghe of the northe, the naked to tene.
The snawe snitered ful snart, that snayped the wylde;
The werbelande wynde wapped fro the hyghe
And drof uche dale ful of dryftes ful grete.
The leude lystened ful wel, that ley in his bedde.
Thagh he lowkes his liddes, ful lyttel he slepes;
Bi uch kok that crue he knwe wel the steven.
Deliverly he dressed up er the day sprenged,
2010 For there was lyght of a laumpe that lemed in his chambre.
He called to his chamberlayn, that cofly hym swared,
And bede hym bryng hym his bruny and his blonk sadel;
That other ferkes hym up and feches hym his wedes,
And graythes me Sir Gawayn upon a grett wyse.
Fyrst he clad hym in his clothes, the colde for to were,
And sythen his other harnays, that holdely was keped,
Bothe his paunce and his plates, piked ful clene,
The rynges rokked of the roust of his riche bruny;
And al was fresch as upon fyrst, and he was fayn thenne
2020   to thonk.
        He hade upon uche pece,

FITT IV

Now night passes and New Year draws near,
drawing off darkness as our Deity decrees.
2000   But wild-looking weather was about in the world:
clouds decanted their cold rain earthwards;
the nithering north needled man's very nature;
creatures were scattered by the stinging sleet.
Then a whip-cracking wind comes whistling between hills
driving snow into deepening drifts in the dales.
Alert and listening, Gawain lies in his bed;
his lids are lowered but he sleeps very little
as each crow of the cock brings his destiny closer.
Before day had dawned he was up and dressed
2010   for the room was livened by the light of a lamp.
To suit him in his metal and to saddle his mount
he called for a servant, who came quickly,
bounded from his bedsheets bringing his garments.
He swathes Sir Gawain in glorious style,
first fastening clothes to fend off the frost,
then his armor, looked after all the while by the household:
the buffed and burnished stomach and breastplates,
and the rings of chain mail, raked free of rust,
all gleaming good as new, for which he is grateful
2020   indeed.
      With every polished piece

Wypped ful wel and wlonk;
The gayest into Grece,
The burne bede bryng his blonk.

Whyle the wlonkest wedes he warp on hymselven—
His cote wyth the conysaunce of the clere werkes
Ennurned upon velvet, vertuus stones
Aboute beten and bounden, enbrauded semes,
And fayre furred withinne wyth fayre pelures—
2030 Yet laft he not the lace, the ladies gifte;
That forgat not Gawayn, for gode of hymselven.
Bi he hade belted the bronde upon his balwe haunches,
Thenn dressed he his drurye double hym aboute,
Swythe swethled umbe his swange swetely that knyght.
The gordel of the grene silke that gay wel bisemed,
Upon that ryol red clothe that ryche was to schewe.
Bot wered not this ilk wyye for wele this gordel,
For pryde of the pendauntes, thagh polyst thay were,
And thagh the glyterande golde glent upon endes,
2040 Bot for to saven hymself when suffer hym byhoved,
To byde bale withoute dabate of bronde hym to were
                    other knyffe.
          Bi that the bolde mon boun
          Wynnes theroute bilyve;
          Alle the meyny of renoun
          He thonkkes ofte ful ryve.

Thenne was Gryngolet graythe, that gret was and huge,
And hade ben sojourned saverly and in a siker wyse;
Hym lyst prik for poynt, that proude hors thenne.
2050 The wyye wynnes hym to and wytes on his lyre,
And sayde soberly hymself and by his soth sweres:

no man shone more, it seemed

from here to ancient Greece.

He sent then for his steed.

He clothes himself in the costliest costume:

his coat with the brightly emblazoned badge

mounted on velvet; magical minerals

inside and set about it; embroidered seams;

a lining finished with fabulous furs. . . .

2030 And he did not leave off the lady's lace girdle;

for his own good, Gawain won't forget that gift.

Then with his sword sheathed at his shapely hips

he bound himself twice about with the belt,

touchingly wrapped it around his waist.

That green silk girdle truly suited Sir Gawain

and went well with the rich red weaves that he wore.

But our man bore the belt not merely for its beauty,

or the appeal of its pennants, polished though they were,

or the gleam of its edges which glimmered with gold,

2040 but to save his skin when presenting himself,

without shield or sword, to the axe. To its swing

               and thwack!

         Now he is geared and gowned

         he steps outside and thinks

         those nobles of renown

         are due his thorough thanks.

Then his great horse Gringolet was got up ready.

The steed had been stabled in comfort and safety

and snorted and stamped in readiness for the ride.

2050 Gawain comes closer to examine his coat,

saying soberly to himself, swearing on his word:

"Here is a meyny in this mote that on menske thenkkes.

The mon hem maynteines, joy mot he have!

The leve lady on lyve, luf hir bityde!

Yif thay for charyté cherysen a gest,

And halden honour in her honde, the hathel hem yelde

That haldes the heven upon hyghe, and also yow alle!

And yif I myght lyf upon londe lede any quyle,

I schuld rech yow sum rewarde redyly, if I myght."

2060　Thenn steppes he into stirop and strydes alofte.

His schalk schewed hym his schelde; on schulder he hit laght,

Gordes to Gryngolet with his gilt heles,

And he startes on the ston—stod he no lenger

        to praunce.

      His hathel on hors was thenne,

      That bere his spere and launce.

      "This kastel to Kryst I kenne:

      He gef hit ay god chaunce!"

The brygge was brayde doun, and the brode yates

2070　Unbarred and born open upon bothe halve.

The burne blessed hym bilyve, and the bredes passed;

Prayses the porter bifore the prynce kneled,

Gef hym God and goud day, that Gawayn he save;

And went on his way with his wyye one,

That schulde teche hym to tourne to that tene place

Ther the ruful race he schulde resayve.

Thay bowen bi bonkkes ther boghes ar bare,

Thay clomben bi clyffes ther clenges the colde.

The heven was up halt, bot ugly therunder;

2080　Mist muged on the mor, malt on the mountes,

Uch hille hade a hatte, a myst hakel huge.

Brokes byled and breke bi bonkkes aboute,

"There are folk in this castle who keep courtesy to the forefront;
their master maintains them—happiness to them all.
And let his lordship's lady be loved all her life.
That they chose, out of charity, to cherish a guest,
showing kindness and care, then may heaven's King
who reigns overall reward them handsomely.
For as long as I live in the lands of this world
I shall practice every means in my power to repay him."
2060 Then he steps in the stirrup and vaults to the saddle
and his servant lifts his shield which he slings on his shoulder,
then he girds on Gringolet with his golden spurs
who clatters from the courtyard, not stalling to snort
           or prance.
      His man was mounted, too,
      who lugged the spear and lance.
      "Christ keep this castle true,"
      he chanted. "Grant good chance."

The drawbridge was dropped, and the double-fronted gates
2070 were unbarred and each half was heaved wide open.
As he clears the planking he crosses himself quickly,
and praises the porter, who kneels before the prince
and prays that God be good to Gawain.
Then he went on his way with the one whose task
was to point out the road to that perilous place
where the knight would receive the slaughterman's strike.
They scrambled up bankings where branches were bare,
clambered up cliff faces crazed by the cold.
The clouds which had climbed now cooled and dropped
2080 so the moors and the mountains were muzzy with mist
and every hill wore a hat of mizzle on its head.
The streams on the slopes seemed to fume and foam,

Schyre schaterande on schores ther thay doun schowved.

Wela wylle was the way ther thay bi wod schulden,

Til hit was sone sesoun that the sunne ryses

that tyde.

Thay were on a hille ful hyghe,

The quyte snaw lay bisyde;

The burne that rod hym by

2090 Bede his mayster abide.

"For I haf wonnen yow hider, wyye, at this tyme,

And now nar ye not fer fro that note place

That ye han spied and spuryed so specially after.

Bot I schal say yow for sothe, sythen I yow knowe,

And ye ar a lede upon lyve that I wel lovy,

Wolde ye worch bi my wytte, ye worthed the better.

The place that ye prece to ful perelous is halden;

Ther wones a wyye in that waste, the worst upon erthe,

For he is stiffe and sturne, and to strike lovies,

2100 And more he is then any mon upon myddelerde,

And his body bigger then the best fowre

That ar in Arthures hous, Hestor, other other.

He cheves that chaunce at the chapel grene,

Ther passes non bi that place so proude in his armes

That he ne dynges hym to dethe with dynt of his honde;

For he is a mon methles, and mercy non uses,

For be hit chorle other chaplayn that bi the chapel rydes,

Monk other masseprest, other any mon elles,

Hym thynk as queme hym to quelle as quyk go hymselven.

2110 Forthy I say the, as sothe as ye in sadel sitte,

Com ye there, ye be kylled, may the knyght rede,

Trawe ye me that trwely, thagh ye had twenty lyves

to spende.

whitening the wayside with spume and spray.

They wandered onwards through the wildest woods

till the sun, at that season, came skyward, showing

> its hand.

> On hilly heights they ride,

> snow littering the land.

> The servant at his side

2090   then has them slow and stand.

"I have accompanied you across this countryside, my lord,

and now we are nearing the site you have named

and have steered and searched for with such singleness of mind.

But there's something I should like to share with you, sir,

because upon my life, you're a lord that I love,

so if you value your health you'll hear my advice:

the place you head for holds a hidden peril.

In that wilderness lives a wildman, the worst in the world,

he is brooding and brutal and loves bludgeoning humans.

2100   He's more powerful than any person alive on this planet

and four times the figure of any fighting knight

in King Arthur's castle, Hector included.

And it's at the green chapel where this grizzliness goes on,

and to pass through that place unscathed is impossible,

for he deals out death blows by dint of his hands,

a man without measure who shows no mercy.

Be it chaplain or churl who rides by his church,

monk or priest, whatever man or person,

he loves murdering more than he loves his own life.

2110   So I say, just as sure as you sit in your saddle,

to find him is fatal, Gawain—that's a fact.

Trust me, he could trample you twenty times over

> or more.

He has wonyd here ful yore,
On bent much baret bende.
Ayayn his dyntes sore
Ye may not yow defende.

"Forthy, goude Sir Gawayn, let the gome one,
And gos away sum other gate, upon Goddes halve!
2120 Cayres bi sum other kyth, ther Kryst mot yow spede.
And I schal hyy me hom ayayn, and hete yow fyrre
That I schal swere bi God and alle his gode halwes—
As help me God and the halydam, and othes innoghe—
That I schal lelly yow layne, and lauce never tale
That ever ye fondet to fle for freke that I wyst."
"Grant merci," quoth Gawayn, and gruchyng he sayde:
"Wel worth the, wyye, that woldes my gode,
And that lelly me layne I leve wel thou woldes.
Bot helde thou hit never so holde, and I here passed,
2130 Founded for ferde for to fle, in fourme that thou telles,
I were a knyght kowarde, I myght not be excused.
Bot I wyl to the chapel, for chaunce that may falle,
And talk wyth that ilk tulk the tale that me lyste,
Worthe hit wele other wo, as the wyrde lykes
          hit hafe.
              Thaghe he be a sturn knape
              To stightel, and stad with stave,
              Ful wel con dryghtyn schape
              His servauntes for to save."

2140 "Mary!" quoth that other mon, "now thou so much spelles
That thou wylt thyn awen nye nyme to thyselven,
And the lyst lese thy lyf, the lette I ne kepe.
Haf here thi helme on thy hede, thi spere in thi honde,

He's lurked about too long
engaged in grief and gore.
His hits are swift and strong—
he'll fell you to the floor."

"So banish that bogeyman to the back of your mind,
and for God's sake travel an alternative track,
2120 ride another road, and be rescued by Christ.
I'll head off home, and with hand on heart
I shall swear by God and all his good saints,
and on all earthly holiness, and other such oaths,
that your secret is safe, and not a soul will know
that you fled in fear from the fellow I described."
"Many thanks," said Gawain, in a terse tone of voice,
"and for having my interests at heart, be lucky.
I'm certain such a secret would be silent in your keep.
But as faithful as you are, if I failed to find him
2130 and lost my mettle in the manner you mentioned,
I'd be christened a coward, and could not be excused.
So I'll trek to the chapel and take my chances,
have it out with that ogre, speak openly to him,
whether fairness or foulness follows, however fate
              behaves.
        He may be stout and stern
        and standing armed with stave,
        but those who strive to serve
        our Lord, our Lord will save."

2140 "By Mary," said the servant, "you seem to be saying
you're hell-bent on heaping harm on yourself
and losing your life, so I'll delay you no longer.
Set your helmet on your head and your lance in your hand

And ryde me doun this ilk rake bi yon rokke syde,

Til thou be broght to the bothem of the brem valay.

Thenne loke a littel on the launde, on thi lyfte honde,

And thou schal se in that slade the self chapel

And the borelych burne on bent that hit kepes.

Now fares wel, on Godes half, Gawayn the noble!

2150   For alle the golde upon grounde I nolde go wyth the,

Ne bere the felawschip thurgh this fryth on fote fyrre."

Bi that the wyye in the wod wendes his brydel,

Hit the hors with the heles as harde as he myght,

Lepes hym over the launde, and leves the knyght there

                    al one,

          "Bi Goddes self," quoth Gawayn,

          "I wyl nauther grete ne grone;

          To Goddes wylle I am ful bayn,

          And to hym I haf me tone."

2160   Thenne gyrdes he to Gryngolet and gederes the rake,

Schowves in bi a schore at a schawe syde,

Rides thurgh the roghe bonk ryght to the dale.

And thenne he wayted hym aboute, and wylde hit hym thoght,

And seye no syngne of resette bisydes nowhere,

Bot hyghe bonkkes and brent upon bothe halve,

And rughe knokled knarres with knorned stones;

The skwes of the scowtes skayned hym thoght.

Thenne he hoved and wythhylde his hors at that tyde,

And ofte chaunged his cher the chapel to seche.

2170   He sey non suche in no syde, and selly hym thoght,

Save a lyttel on a launde, a lawe as hit were,

A balw berw bi a bonke the brymme bysyde,

Bi a fors of a flode that ferked thare;

and ride a route through that rocky ravine
till you're brought to the bottom of that foreboding valley,
then look towards a glade a little to the left
and you'll see in the clearing the site itself,
and the hulking superhuman who inhabits the place.
Now God bless and good-bye, brave Sir Gawain;
for all the wealth in the world I wouldn't walk with you
or go further in this forest by a single footstep."
With a wrench on the reins he reeled around
and heel-kicked the horse as hard as he could,
and was gone from Gawain, galloping hard
        for home.
      "By Christ, I will not cry,"
      announced the knight, "or groan,
      but find good fortune by
      the grace of God alone."

Then he presses ahead, picks up a path,
enters a steep-sided grove on his steed
then goes by and by to the bottom of a gorge
where he wonders and watches—it looks a wild place:
no sign of a settlement anywhere to be seen
but heady heights to both halves of the valley
and set with saber-toothed stones of such sharpness
no cloud in the sky could escape unscratched.
He stalls and halts, holds the horse still,
glances side to side to glimpse the green chapel
but sees no such thing, which he thinks is strange,
except at mid-distance what might be a mound,
a sort of bald knoll on the bank of a brook
where fell water surged with frenzied force,

The borne blubred therinne as hit boyled hade,

The knyght kaches his caple and com to the lawe,

Lightes doun luflyly, and at a lynde taches

The rayne and his riche with a roghe braunche.

Thenne he bowes to the berwe, aboute hit he walkes,

Debatande with hymself quat hit be myght.

2180 Hit hade a hole on the ende and on ayther syde,

And overgrowen with gresse in glodes aywhere;

And al was holw inwith, nobot an olde cave,

Or a crevisse of an olde cragge—he couthe hit noght deme

with spelle.

"We! Lorde," quoth the gentyle knyght,

"Whether this be the grene chapelle?

Here myght aboute mydnyght

The dele his matynnes telle!

"Now iwysse," quoth Wowayn, "wysty is here;

2190 This oritore is ugly, with erbes overgrowen;

Wel bisemes the wyye wruxled in grene

Dele here his devocioun on the develes wyse.

Now I fele hit is the fende, in my fyve wyttes,

That has stoken me this steven to strye me here.

This is a chapel of meschaunce—that chekke hit bytyde!

Hit is the corsedest kyrk that ever I com inne."

With heghe helme on his hede, his launce in his honde,

He romes up to the roffe of tho rogh wones.

Thene herde he of that hyghe hil, in a harde roche

2200 Biyonde the broke, in a bonk, a wonder breme noyse.

Quat! hit clatered in the clyff as hit cleve schulde,

As one upon a gryndelston hade grounden a sythe.

What! hit wharred and whette, as water at a mulne.

What! hit rusched and ronge, rawthe to here.

bursting with bubbles as if it had boiled.
He heels the horse, heads for that mound,
grounds himself gracefully and tethers Gringolet,
looping the reins to the limb of a lime.
Then he strides forwards and circles the feature,
baffled as to what that bizarre hill could be:
2180　it had a hole at one end and at either side,
and its walls, matted with weeds and moss,
enclosed a cavity, like a kind of old cave
or crevice in the crag—it was all too unclear to
　　　　　　　declare.
　　　　　"Green Church?" chunters the knight.
　　　　　"More like the devil's lair
　　　　　where, at the nub of night,
　　　　　he makes his morning prayer."

　　　　　"For certain," he says, "this is a soulless spot,
2190　a ghostly cathedral overgrown with grass,
the kind of kirk where that camouflaged man
might deal in devilment and all things dark.
My five senses inform me that Satan himself
has tricked me in this tryst, intending to destroy me.
This is a haunted house—may it go to hell.
I never came across a church so cursed."
With head helmeted and lance in hand
he scrambled to the skylight of that strange abyss.
Then he heard on the hillside, from behind a hard rock
2200　and beyond the brook, a blood-chilling noise.
What! It cannoned though the cliffs as if they might crack,
like the scream of a scythe being ground on a stone.
What! It whined and wailed, like a waterwheel.
What! It rasped and rang, raw on the ear.

Thenne "Bi Godde," quoth Gawayn, "that gere, as I trowe,
Is ryched at the reverence me, renk to mete
                        bi rote.
            Let God worche! 'We loo'—
            Hit helppes me not a mote.
2210   My lif thagh I forgoo,
            Drede dos me no lote."

Thenne the knyght con calle ful hyghe:
"Who stightles in this sted, me steven to holde?
For now is gode Gawayn goande ryght here.
If any wyye oght wyl, wynne hider fast,
Other now other never, his nedes to spede."
"Abyde," quoth on on the bonke aboven over his hede,
"And thou schal haf al in hast that I the hyght ones."
Yet he rusched on that rurde rapely a throwe,
2220 And wyth quettyng awharf, er he wolde lyght.
And sythen he keveres bi a cragge and comes of a hole,
Whyrlande out of a wro wyth a felle weppen,
A denes ax nwe dyght, the dynt with to yelde,
With a borelych bytte bende by the halme,
Fyled in a fylor, fowre fote large—
Hit was no lasse, bi that lace that lemed ful bryght.
And the gome in the grene gered as fyrst,
Bothe the lyre and the legges, lokkes and berde,
Save that fayre on his fote he foundes on the erthe,
2230 Sette the stele to the stone and stalked bysyde.
When he wan to the watter, ther he wade nolde,
He hypped over on hys ax and orpedly strydes,
Bremly brothe, on a bent that brode was aboute,
                        on snawe.

"My God," cried Gawain, "that grinding is a greeting.
My arrival is honored with the honing of an axe
        up there.
     Then let the Lord decide.
     'Oh well,' won't help me here.
2210   I might well lose my life
     but freak sounds hold no fear."

Then Gawain called as loudly as his lungs would allow,
"Who has power in this place to honor his pact?
Because good Gawain now walks on this ground.
Whoever will meet him should emerge this moment
and he needs to be fast—it's now or it's never."
"Abide," came a voice from above the bank.
"You'll cop for what's coming to you quickly enough."
Yet he went at his work, whetting the blade,
2220 not showing until it was sharpened and stropped.
Then out of the crags he comes, through the cave mouth,
whirling into view with a wondrous weapon,
a Danish-style axe for doling out death,
with a brute of a blade curving back to the haft
filed on a stone, a four footer at least
by the look of the length of its shining lace.
And again he was green, like a year ago,
with green hair and flesh and a fully green face,
and firmly on green feet he came stomping forwards,
2230 the handle of that axe like a staff in his hand.
At the edge of the water he will not wade
but vaults the stream with the shaft, and strides
with an ominous face onto earth covered over
        with snow.

Sir Gawayn the knyght con mete,
He ne lutte hym nothyng lowe;
That other sayde: "Now, sir swete,
Of steven mon may the trowe.

"Gawayn," quoth that grene gome, "God the mot loke!
2240 Iwysse thou art welcom, wyye, to my place,
And thou has tymed thi travayl as truee mon schulde.
And thou knowes the covenauntes kest uus bytwene:
At this tyme twelmonyth thou toke that the falled,
And I schulde at this Nwe Yere yeply the quyte.
And we ar in this valay verayly oure one;
Here ar no renkes us to rydde, rele as uus likes.
Haf thy helme of thy hede, and haf here thy pay.
Busk no more debate then I the bede thenne
When thou wypped of my hede at a wap one."
2250 "Nay, bi God," quoth Gawayn, "that me gost lante,
I schal gruch the no grwe for grem that falles.
Bot styghtel the upon on strok, and I schal stonde stylle
And warp the no wernyng to worch as the lykes,
                    nowhare."
            He lened with the nek, and lutte,
            And schewed that schyre al bare,
            And lette as he noght dutte;
            For drede he wolde not dare.

Then the gome in the grene graythed hym swythe,
2260 Gederes up hys grymme tole, Gawayn to smyte;
With alle the bur in his body he ber hit on lofte,
Munt as maghtyly as marre hym he wolde.
Hade hit dryven adoun as drey as he atled,

Our brave knight bowed, his head
hung low—but not too low!
"Young Sir," the green man said,
"Your visit keeps your vow."

The green knight spoke again, "God guard you, Gawain.
2240   Welcome to my world after all your wandering.
You have timed your arrival like a true traveler
to begin this business which binds us together.
Last year, at this time, what was yielded became yours,
and with New Year come you are called to account.
We're very much alone, beyond view in this valley,
no person to part us—we can do as we please.
Pull your helmet from your head and take what you're owed.
Show no more struggle than I showed myself
when you severed my spine with a single smite."
2250   "No," said good Gawain, "by my life-giving God,
I won't gripe or begrudge the grimness to come,
so keep to one stroke and I'll stand stock-still,
won't whisper a word of unwillingness, or one
                 complaint."
           He bowed to take the blade
           and bared his neck and nape,
           but, loath to look afraid,
           he feigned a fearless state.

Suddenly the green knight summons up his strength,
2260   hoists the axe high over Gawain's head,
lifts it aloft with every fiber of his life
and begins to bring home a bone-splitting blow.
Had he seen it through as thoroughly as threatened

Ther hade ben ded of his dynt that doghty was ever.

Bot Gawayn on that giserne glyfte hym bysyde,

As hit com glydande adoun on glode hym to schende,

And schranke a lytel with the schulderes for the scharp yrne.

That other schalk wyth a schunt the schene wythhaldes,

And thenne repreved he the prynce with mony prowde wordes:

2270 "Thou art not Gawayn," quoth the gome, "that is so goud halden,

That never arwed for no here by hylle ne be vale,

And now thou fles for ferde er thou fele harmes.

Such cowardise of that knyght cowthe I never here.

Nawther fyked I ne flaghe, freke, quen thou myntest,

Ne kest no kavelacion in kynges hous Arthor.

My hede flaw to my fote, and yet flagh I never;

And thou, er any harme hent, arwes in hert.

Wherfore the better burne me burde be called

                    therfore."

2280   Quoth Gawayn: "I schunt ones,

                 And so wyl I no more;

                 Bot thagh my hede falle on the stones,

                 I con not hit restore.

"Bot busk, burne, bi thi fayth, and bryng me to the poynt.

Dele to me my destiné and do hit out of honde,

For I schal stonde the a strok, and start no more

Til thyn ax have me hitte—haf here my trawthe."

"Haf at the thenne," quoth that other, and heves hit alofte,

And waytes as wrothely as he wode were.

2290 He myntes at hym maghtyly, bot not the mon rynes,

Withhelde heterly his honde er hit hurt myght.

Gawayn graythely hit bydes and glent with no membre,

Bot stode stylle as the ston other a stubbe auther

That ratheled is in roché grounde with rotes a hundreth.

the man beneath him would have met with his maker.
But glimpsing the axe at the edge of his eye
bringing death earthwards as it arced through the air,
and sensing its sharpness, Gawain shrank at the shoulders.
The swinging axman swerved from his stroke,
and reproached the young prince with piercing words:

2270 "Call yourself good Sir Gawain?" he goaded,
"who faced down every foe in the field of battle
but now flinches with fear at the foretaste of harm.
Never have I known such a namby-pamby knight.
Did I budge or even blink when you aimed the axe,
or carp or quibble in King Arthur's castle,
or flap when my head went flying to my feet?
But entirely untouched, you are terror struck.
I'll be found the better fellow, since you were so feeble
                    and frail."

2280   Gawain confessed, "I flinched
                at first, but will not fail.
                Though once my head's unhitched
                it's off once and for all!"

"So be brisk with the blow, bring on the blade.
Deal me my destiny and do it out of hand,
and I'll stand the stroke without shiver or shudder
and be wasted by your weapon. You have my word."
"Take this then," said the other, throwing up the axe,
menacing the young man with the gaze of a maniac.

2290 Then he launches his swing but leaves him unscathed,
withholds his arm before harm could be done.
And Gawain was motionless, never moved a muscle,
but stood stone-still, or as still as a tree stump
anchored in the earth by a hundred roots.

Then muryly efte con he mele, the mon in the grene:

"So now thou has thi hert holle, hitte me bihoves.

Halde the now the hyghe hode that Arthur the raght,

And kepe thy kanel at this kest, yif hit kever may!"

Gawayn ful gryndelly with greme thenne sayde:

2300 "Wy, thresch on, thou thro mon, thou thretes to longe;

I hope that thi hert arwe wyth thyn awen selven."

"For sothe," quoth that other freke, "so felly thou spekes,

I wyl no lenger on lyte lette thin ernde

right nowe."

Thenne tas he hym strythe to stryke

And frounses bothe lyppe and browe;

No mervayle thagh hym myslyke

That hoped of no rescowe.

He lyftes lyghtly his lome and let hit doun fayre,

2310 With the barbe of the bitte bi the bare nek.

Thagh he homered heterly, hurt hym no more,

Bot snyrt hym on that on syde, that severed the hyde.

The scharp schrank to the flesche thurgh the schyre grece,

That the schene blod over his schulderes schot to the erthe.

And quen the burne sey the blode blenk on the snawe,

He sprit forth spenne-fote more then a spere lenthe,

Hent heterly his helme and on his hed cast,

Schot with his schulderes his fayre schelde under,

Braydes out a bryght sworde, and bremely he spekes—

2320 Never syn that he was burne borne of his moder

Was he never in this worlde wyye half so blythe—

"Blynne, burne, of thy bur, bede me no mo!

I haf a stroke in this sted withoute stryf hent,

And if thow reches me any mo, I redyly schal quyte

Then the warrior in green mocked Gawain again:
"Now you've plucked up your courage I'll dispatch you properly.
May the honorable knighthood heaped on you by Arthur—
if it proves to be powerful—protect your pretty neck."
That insulting slur drew a spirited response:

2300 "Get hacking, then, head-banger, your threats are hollow.
Such huffing and fussing—you'll frighten your own heart."
"By God," said the green man, "since you speak so grandly
there'll be no more shilly-shallying, I shall shatter you
                right now."
            He stands to strike, a sneer
            from bottom lip to brow.
            Who'd fault Gawain if fear
            took hold. All hope is down.

Hoisted and aimed, the axe hurtled downwards,
2310 the blade baring down on the knight's bare neck,
a ferocious blow, but far from being fatal
it skewed to one side, just skimming the skin
and finely snicking the fat of the flesh
so that bright red blood shot from body to earth.
Seeing it shining on the snowy ground
Gawain leapt forward a spear's length at least,
grabbed hold of his helmet and rammed it on his head,
brought his shield to his side with a shimmy of his shoulder,
then brandished his sword before blurting out brave words,
2320 because never since birth, as his mother's babe,
was he half as happy as here and now.
"Enough swiping, sir, you've swung your last swing.
I've borne one blow without backing out,
go for me again and you'll get some by return,

And yelde yederly ayayn—and therto ye tryst—
                    and foo.
              Bot on stroke here me falles;
              The covenaunt schop ryght so,
              Festned in Arthures halles,
2330   And therfore, hende, now hoo!"

The hathel heldet hym fro and on his ax rested,
Sette the schaft upon schore and to the scharp lened,
And loked to the leude that on the launde yede,
How that doghty, dredles, dervely ther stondes
Armed, ful awles; in hert hit hym lykes.
Thenn he meles muryly wyth a much steven,
And wyth a rynkande rurde he to the renk sayde:
"Bolde burne, on this bent be not so gryndel.
No mon here unmanerly the mysboden habbes,
2340 Ne kyd bot as covenaunde at kynges kort schaped.
I hyght the a strok and thou hit has, halde the wel payed;
I relece the of the remnaunt of ryghtes alle other.
Iif I deliver had bene, a boffet paraunter
I couthe wrotheloker haf waret, to the haf wroght anger.
Fyrst I mansed the muryly with a mynt one,
And rove the wyth no rof sore, with ryght I the profered
For the forwarde that we fest in the fyrst nyght;
And thou trystyly the trawthe and trwly me haldes,
Al the gayne thow me gef, as god mon schulde.
2350 That other munt for the morne, mon, I the profered;
Thou kyssedes my clere wyf, the cosses me raghtes.
For bothe two here I the bede bot two bare myntes
                    boute scathe.
              Trwe mon trwe restore,
              Thenne thar mon drede no wathe.

with interest! Hit out, and be hit in an instant,
        and hard.
      One axe attack—that's all.
      Now keep the covenant
      agreed in Arthur's hall
2330   and hold the axe in hand."

The warrior steps away and leans on his weapon,
props the handle in the earth and slouches on the head
and studies how Gawain is standing his ground,
bold in his bearing, brave in his actions,
armed and ready. In his heart he admires him.
With volume but less violence in his voice, he replied
with reaching words which rippled and rang:
"Be a mite less feisty, fearless young fellow,
no insulting or heinous incident has happened
2340 beyond the game we agreed on in the court of your king.
One strike was promised—consider it served!
From any lingering loyalties you are hereby released.
Had I mustered all my muscles into one mighty blow
my axe would have dealt you your death, without doubt.
But my first strike fooled you—a feint, no less—
not fracturing your flesh, which was only fair
in keeping with the contract we declared that first night,
for with truthful behavior you honored my trust
and gave up your gains as a good man should.
2350 Then I missed you once more, and this for the morning
when you kissed my pretty wife then kindly kissed me.
So twice you were truthful, therefore twice I left
        no scar.
      The person who repays
      will live to feel no fear.

At the thrid thou fayled thore,
And therfor that tappe ta the.

For hit is my wede that thou weres, that ilke woven girdel;
Myn owen wyf hit the weved, I wot wel for sothe.
2360   Now know I wel thy cosses and thy costes als,
And the wowyng of my wyf; I wroght hit myselven.
I sende hir to asay the, and sothly me thynkkes
On the fautlest freke that ever on fote yede.
As perle bi the quite pese is of prys more,
So is Gawayn, in god fayth, bi other gay knyghtes.
Bot here yow lakked a lyttel, sir, and lewté yow wonted;
Bot that was for no wylyde werke, ne wowyng nauther,
Bot for ye lufed your lyf—the lasse I yow blame."
That other stif mon in study stod a gret whyle,
2370   So agreved for greme he gryed withinne.
Alle the blode of his brest blende in his face,
That al he schrank for schome that the schalk talked.
The forme worde upon folde that the freke meled:
"Corsed worth cowarddyse and covetyse bothe!
In yow is vylany and vyse that vertue disstryes."
Thenne he kaght to the knot and the kest lawses,
Brayde brothely the belt to the burne selven:
"Lo! ther the falssyng, foule mot hit falle!
For care of thy knokke cowardyse me taght
2380   To acorde me with covetyse, my kynde to forsake,
That is larges and lewté that longes to knyghtes.
Now am I fawty and falce, and ferde haf ben ever;
Of trecherye and untrawthe bothe bityde sorwe
          and care!
      I biknowe yow, knyght, here stylle,
      Al fawty is my fare;

The third time, though, you strayed,
and felt my blade therefore."

"Because the belt you are bound with belongs to me;
it was woven by my wife so I know it very well.
2360 And I know of your courtesies, and conduct, and kisses,
and the wooing of my wife—for it was all my work!
I sent her to test you—and in truth it turns out
you're by the far the most faultless fellow on earth.
As a pearl is more prized than a pea which is white,
so, by God, is Gawain, amongst gallant knights.
But a little thing more—it was loyalty that you lacked:
not because you're wicked, or a womanizer, or worse,
but you loved your own life; so I blame you less."
Gawain stood speechless for what seemed like a century,
2370 so shocked and ashamed that his stomach churned
and the fire of his blood brought flames to his face
and he wriggled and writhed at the other man's words.
Then he tried to talk, and finding his tongue, said:
"A curse upon cowardice and covetousness.
They breed villainy and vice, and destroy all virtue."
Then he grabbed the girdle and ungathered its knot
and flung it in fury at the man in front.
"My downfall and undoing; let the devil take it.
Dread of the death blow and cowardly doubts
2380 meant I gave in to greed, and in doing so forgot
the fidelity and kindness which every knight knows.
As I feared, I am found to be flawed and false,
through treachery and untruth I have totally failed," said
          Gawain.
          "Such terrible mistakes,
          and I shall bear the blame.

Letes me overtake your wylle,
And efte I schal be ware."

Thenn loghe that other leude and luflyly sayde:
2390 "I halde hit hardily hole, the harme that I hade;
Thou art confessed so clene, beknowen of thy mysses,
And has the penaunce apert of the poynt of myn egge.
I halde the polysed of that plyght and pured as clene
As thou hades never forfeted sythen thou was fyrst borne.
And I gif the, sir, the gurdel that is golde-hemmed.
For hit is grene as my goune, Sir Gawayn, ye maye
Thenk upon this ilke threpe ther thou forth thrynges
Among prynces of prys, and this a pure token
Of the chaunce of the grene chapel at chevalrous knyghtes.
2400 And ye schal in this Nwe Yer ayayn to my wones,
And we schyn revel the remnaunt of this ryche fest
        ful bene."
            Ther lathed hym fast the lorde,
            And sayde: "With my wyf, I wene,
            We schal yow wel acorde,
            That was your enmy kene."

"Nay, for sothe," quoth the segge, and sesed hys helme
And has hit of hendely, and the hathel thonkkes:
"I haf sojorned sadly. Sele yow bytyde,
2410 And he yelde hit yow yare that yarkkes al menskes!
And comaundes me to that cortays, your comlych fere,
Bothe that on and that other, myn honoured ladyes,
That thus hor knyght wyth hor kest han koyntly bigyled.
Bot hit is no ferly thagh a fole madde
And thurgh wyles of wymmen be wonen to sorwe.
For so was Adam in erde with one bygyled,

But tell me what it takes
to clear my clouded name."

The green lord laughed, and leniently replied:
2390 "The harm which you caused me is wholly healed.
By confessing your failings you are free from fault
and have openly paid penance at the point of my axe.
I declare you purged, as polished and as pure
as the day you were born, without blemish or blame.
And this gold-hemmed girdle I present as a gift,
which is green like my gown. It's yours, Sir Gawain,
a reminder of our meeting when you mix and mingle
with princes and kings. And this keepsake will be proof
to all chivalrous knights of your challenge in this chapel.
2400 But follow me home. New Year's far from finished—
we'll resume our reveling with supper and song.
         What's more
      my wife is waiting there
      who flummoxed you before.
      This time you'll have in her
      a friend and not a foe."

"Thank you," said the other, taking helmet from head,
holding it in hand as he offered his thanks.
"But I've loitered long enough. The Lord bless your life
2410 and bestow on you such honor as you surely deserve.
And mind you commend me to your mannerly wife,
both to her and the other, those honorable ladies
who kidded me so cleverly with their cunning tricks.
But no wonder if a fool should fall for a female
and be wiped of his wits by womanly guile—
it's the way of the world. Adam fell for a woman

And Salamon with fele sere, and Samson eftsones—
Dalyda dalt hym hys wyrde—and Davyth therafter
Was blended with Barsabe, that much bale tholed.
2420 Now these were wrathed wyth her wyles, hit were a wynne huge
To luf hom wel and leve hem not, a leude that couthe.
For thes wer forne the freest, that folwed alle the sele
Exellently of alle thyse other under hevenryche
                    that mused;
           And alle thay were biwyled
           With wymmen that thay used.
           Thagh I be now bigyled,
           Me think me burde be excused.

"Bot your gordel," quoth Gawayn, "God yow foryelde!
2430 That wyl I welde wyth guod wylle, not for the wynne golde,
Ne the saynt, ne the sylk, ne the syde pendaundes,
For wele ne for worchyp, ne for the wlonk werkkes;
Bot in syngne of my surfet I schal se hit ofte
When I ride in renoun, remorde to myselven
The faut and the fayntyse of the flesche crabbed,
How tender hit is to entyse teches of fylthe.
And thus quen pryde schal me pryk for prowes of armes,
The loke to this luf-lace schal lethe my hert.
Bot on I wolde yow pray, displeses yow never:
2440 Syn ye be lorde of the yonde londe ther I haf lent inne
Wyth yow wyth worschyp—the wyye hit yow yelde
That uphaldes the heven and on hygh sittes—
How norne ye yowre ryght nome, and thenne no more?"
"That schal I telle the trwly," quoth that other thenne,
"Bertilak de Hautdesert I hat in this londe.
Thurgh myght of Morgne la Faye, that in my hous lenges,

and Solomon for several, and as for Samson,
Delilah was his downfall, and afterwards David
was bamboozled by Bathsheba and bore the grief.
2420 All wrecked and ruined by their wrongs; if only
we could love our ladies without believing their lies.
And those were fellows from fortunate families,
excellent beyond all others existing under heaven,"
                    he cried.
            "Yet all were charmed and changed
            by wily womankind.
            I suffered just the same,
            so clear me of my crime."

"But the girdle," he went on, "God bless you for this gift.
2430 Not for all its ore will I own it with honor,
nor its silks and streamers, and not for the sake
of its wonderful workmanship or even its worth,
but as a sign of my sin—I'll see it as such
when I swagger in the saddle—a sad reminder
that the frailty of his flesh is man's biggest fault,
how the touch of filth taints his tender frame.
When my pulse races with passion and pride
one look at this love-lace will lessen my ardor.
But I will ask one thing, if it won't offend:
2440 since I spent so long in your lordship's land
and was hosted in your house—let Him reward you
who upholds the heavens and sits upon high—
will you make known your name? And I'll ask nothing else."
"Then I'll treat you to the truth," the other told him,
"Here in my homelands they call me Bertilak de Hautdesert.
And in my manor lives the mighty Morgan le Fay,

And koyntyse of clergye, bi craftes wel lerned.

The maystrés of Merlyn, mony ho has taken,

For ho has dalt drwry ful dere sumtyme

2450 With that conable klerk, that knowes alle your knyghtes

at hame.

Morgne the goddes

Therfore hit is hir name;

Weldes non so hyghe hawtesse

That ho ne con make ful tame.

Ho wayned me upon this wyse to your wynne halle

For to assay the surquidré, yif hit soth were

That rennes of the grete renoun of the Rounde Table.

Ho wayned me this wonder your wyttes to reve,

2460 For to haf greved Gaynour and gart hir to dyye

With glopnyng of that ilke gome that gostlych speked

With his hede in his honde bifore the hyghe table.

That is ho that is at home, the auncian lady;

Ho is even thyn aunt, Arthures half-suster,

The duches doghter of Tyntagelle, that dere Vter after

Hade Arthur upon, that athel is nowthe.

Therfore I ethe the, hathel, to com to thy naunt,

Make myry in my hous. My meny the lovies,

And I wol the as wel, wyye, bi my faythe,

2470 As any gome under God, for thy grete trauthe."

And he nikked hym naye, he nolde bi no wayes.

Thay acolen and kyssen, bykennen ayther other

To the prynce of paradise, and parten ryght there

on coolde.

Gawayn on blonk ful bene

To the kynges burgh buskes bolde,

so adept and adroit in the dark arts,
who learned magic from Merlin—the master of mystery—
for in earlier times she was intimately entwined
2450 with that knowledgeable man, as all you knights know
                    back home.
            Yes, 'Morgan the Goddess'—
            I will announce her name.
            There is no nobleness
            she cannot take and tame."

"She guided me in this guise to your great hall
to put pride on trial, and to test with this trick
what distinction and trust the Round Table deserves.
She imagined this mischief would muddle your minds
2460 and that grieving Guinevere would go to her grave
at the sight of a specter making ghostly speeches
with his head in his hands before the high table.
So that ancient woman who inhabits my home
is also your aunt—Arthur's half sister,
the daughter of the duchess of Tintagel; the duchess
who through Uther, was mother to Arthur, your king.
So I ask you again, come and greet your aunt
and make merry in my house; you're much loved there,
by me more than most, for as God be my maker
2470 your word holds more worth than most anyone in this world."
But Gawain would not. No way would he go.
So they clasped and kissed and made kindly commendations
to the Prince of Paradise, and then parted in the cold,
                that pair.
            Our man, back on his mount
            now hurtles home from there.

And the knyght in the enker grene
Whiderwarde-so-ever he wolde.

Wylde wayes in the worlde Wowen now rydes
2480 On Gryngolet, that the grace hade geten of his lyve.
Ofte he herbered in house and ofte al theroute,
And mony aventure in vale, and venquyst ofte,
That I ne tyght at this tyme in tale to remene.
The hurt was hole that he hade hent in his nek,
And the blykkande belt he bere theraboute,
Abelef as a bauderyk, bounden bi his syde,
Loken under his lyfte arme, the lace, with a knot,
In tokenyng he was tane in tech of a faute.
And thus he commes to the court, knyght al in sounde.
2490 Ther wakned wele in that wone when wyst the grete
That gode Gawayn was commen; gayn hit hym thoght.
The kyng kysses the knyght, and the whene alce,
And sythen mony syker knyght that soght hym to haylce,
Of his fare that hym frayned; and ferlyly he telles,
Biknowes alle the costes of care that he hade—
The chaunce of the chapel, the chere of the knyght,
The luf of the ladi, the lace at the last.
The nirt in the nek he naked hem schewed,
That he laght for his unleuté at the leudes hondes
2500   for blame.
       He tened quen he schulde telle,
       He groned for gref and grame;
       The blod in his face con melle,
       When he hit schulde schewe, for schame.

"Lo! lorde," quoth the leude, and the lace hondeled,
"This is the bende of this blame I bere on my nek,

The green knight leaves his ground
to wander who-knows-where.

So he winds through the wilds of the world once more,
2480   Gawain on Gringolet, by the grace of God,
under a roof sometimes and sometimes roughing it,
and in valleys and vales had adventures and victories
but time is too tight to tell how they went.
The nick to his neck was healed by now;
thereabouts he had bound the belt like a baldric—
slantwise, as a sash, from shoulder to side,
laced in a knot looped below his left arm,
a sign that his honor was stained by sin.
So safe and sound he sets foot in court,
2490   and when clansmen had learned of their comrade's return
happiness cannoned through the echoing halls.
The king kissed his knight and so did the queen,
and Gawain was embraced by his band of brothers,
who made eager enquiries, and he answered them all
with the tale of his trial and tribulations,
and the challenge at the chapel, and the great green chap,
and the love of the lady, which led to the belt.
And he showed them the scar at the side of his neck,
confirming his breach of faith, like a badge
2500   of blame.
He grimaced with disgrace,
he writhed in rage and pain.
Blood flowed towards his face
and showed his smarting shame.

"Regard," said Gawain, grabbing the girdle,
"through this I suffered a scar to my skin—

This is the lathe and the losse that I laght have

Of couardise and covetyse that I haf caght thare.

This is the token of untrawthe that I am tan inne,

2510 And I mot nedes hit were wyle I may last.

For non may hyden his harme bot unhap ne may hit,

For ther hit ones is tachched twynne wil hit never."

The kyng comfortes the knyght, and alle the court als,

Laghen loude therat, and luflyly acorden

That lordes and ladis that longed to the Table,

Uche burne of the brotherhede, a bauderyk schulde have,

A bende abelef hym aboute, of a bryght grene,

And that, for sake of that segge, in swete to were.

For that was acorded the renoun of the Rounde Table,

2520 And he honoured that hit hade, evermore after,

As hit is breved in the best boke of romaunce.

Thus in Arthurus day this aunter bitidde,

The Brutus bokes therof beres wyttenesse.

Sythen Brutus, the bolde burne, bowed hider fyrst,

After the segge and the asaute was sesed at Troye,

iwysse,

Mony aunteres here-biforne

Haf fallen suche er this.

Now that bere the croun of thorne,

2530 He bryng uus to his blysse! AMEN.

HONY SOYT QUI MAL PENCE

for my loss of faith I was physically defaced;
what a coveting coward I became it would seem.
I was tainted by untruth and this, its token,
2510 I will drape across my chest till the day I die.
For man's crimes can be covered but never made clean;
once entwined with sin, man is twinned for all time."
The king gave comfort, then laughter filled the castle
and in friendly accord the company of the court
allowed that each lord belonging to their Order—
every knight in the brotherhood—should bear such a belt,
a bright green belt worn obliquely to the body,
crosswise, like a sash, for the sake of this man.
So that slanting green stripe was adopted as their sign,
2520 and each knight who held it was honored forever,
as all meaningful writings on romance remind us:
an adventure which happened in the era of Arthur,
as the chronicles of this country have stated clearly.
Since fearless Brutus first set foot
on these shores, once the siege and assault at Troy
          had ceased,
          our coffers have been crammed
          with stories such as these.
          Now let our Lord, thorn-crowned,
2530   bring us to perfect peace. AMEN.

HONY SOYT QUI MAL PENCE

ΛCKNOWLEÐGΠΕΝΤS

I can't pinpoint the moment when I decided to translate *Sir Gawain,* or remember how and why the idea came to me. A series of coincidences, probably. Like noticing my wife's dog-eared copy of the Tolkien and Gordon edition, the "green book," poking out of the bookshelf. Then leafing through it and my eye falling on a particular word—"wodwo"—a word well known to readers of Ted Hughes. Then the poem coming up in a conversation with the poet Glyn Maxwell in a taxi in Poland, who'd been reviewing a new version of *Gawain.* Then remembering that Hughes himself had translated several sections of the poem, and going back to read them, then remembering Tolkien's translation, which I'd read about twenty years ago, with its highly wrought sentences and ornate diction. Taken on their own, none of these incidents and recollections would have amounted to anything much, but when taken together they seemed like some kind of BIG HINT. Here was a narrative poem, one reliant upon craft and technique, written in a nonmetropolitan voice. Within about a week, the idea had gone from a fanciful notion to a superstitious (and preposterous) conviction that I was put on the planet for no other reason than to work on this poem.

This translation was first commissioned by Faber & Faber in the UK then shortly afterward by W. W. Norton in the United States. I am thankful to Seamus Heaney for his initial enthusiasm and support. From my position, Heaney's *Beowulf* and Ted Hughes's *Tales of*

Ovid are like two monumental gateposts standing ahead of any poet wishing to travel in this particular direction. The writing was begun in mid 2003 and completed late in 2007. Even at proof stage, amendments and corrections were still being made, and the often-quoted notion that a poem can never be finished, only abandoned, has never felt more true. Even now, further permutations and possibilities keep suggesting themselves, as if the tweaking and fine-tuning could last a lifetime. I am grateful to my editor at Faber, Paul Keegan, for his many pages of remarks and for finally declaring the writing to be at an end, and to Charles Boyle for putting up with my faffing and fiddling. Large thanks are also due to Professor James Simpson at Harvard University for his overview of the Norton edition of this translation, and for raising an eyebrow at some of my wilder notions, even from two and a half thousand miles away.

The Tolkien and Gordon edition of *Sir Gawain and the Green Knight,* revised by Norman Davies (Oxford 1967), with its plain-speaking commentary and extensive glossary, provided the foundation text for this project, along with the Everyman (1976) edition of A. C. Cawley and J. J. Anderson (used here in parallel), Malcolm Andrew and Ronald Waldron's edition published by University of Exeter Press, and the edition of J. A. Burrow (Penguin 1972). Notable and inspiring translations (with their indispensable notes and insights) include those of J. R. R. Tolkien (Allen & Unwin 1975; published in the United States by Houghton Mifflin), Brian Stone (Penguin 1959), Keith Harrison (Oxford 1983), W. R. J. Barron (University of Manchester 1974) and very recently that of fellow poet Bernard O'Donoghue (Penguin 2006). As a motivation to my own approach, I would especially mention the translation by Marie Borroff (Norton 1967), with its insistence on meter and rhyme where appropriate, and its dedication to upholding the alliterative drive of the original. *A Companion to the Gawain Poet* (ed. Derek Brewer, Cambridge 1997) is an important and useful critical anthology, as is J. A. Burrow and

Thorlac Turville-Petre's *A Book of Middle English* (Blackwell 1992). Thank you to Peter Davidson at The University of Aberdeen for his cheery comments and useful connections, and to Peter Kidd at the British Library for arranging a long-anticipated viewing of the original manuscript. Prior to that, and in lieu of the real thing, the Early English Text Society's 1923 facsimile edition, introduced by I. Gollancz, was a more than adequate substitute.

about the gawain poet

The identity of the author of *Sir Gawain and the Green Knight* is not known. Only a single copy of the poem survives, bound in a manuscript with three other poems. Like the *Gawain* poem they bear no specific title but have come to be known as *Pearl, Cleanness,* and *Patience.* Scholarship tells us that all four poems were probably composed by the same person. The manuscript also contains twelve simple but intriguing illustrations of which four relate to moments in the *Gawain* story. Many other immaculately preserved ancient texts appear hardly to have been opened, let alone read. But the *Gawain* manuscript has been well thumbed over the centuries, and seems to have been put to the task it was intended on many occasions.

The person who inscribed the poem was not its author. The *Gawain* poet, or the *Pearl* poet as he is sometimes called, was probably an educated man living and writing in the late part of the fourteenth century. His eclectic, almost eccentric vocabulary distinguishes him from other authors of the Middle English period. He was familiar with the stories of Arthurian Romance, and might also have been aware that some elements within his story, such as the beheading motif, could be traced back to early Irish literature. He would have been a contemporary of Chaucer, though we know from the language of the poem that he was not a Londoner but from somewhere further north. Dialect words in the poem suggest an imprecise area around

Staffordshire, Cheshire, Derbyshire, or Lancashire. The geography of the poem, such as that of North Wales and the Wirral, along with other recognizable topographies are further evidence of the *Gawain* poet's "regional" background. In trying to establish his identity, one line of enquiry has been to look for numerological clues within the text (a common practice within medieval writings), for example by matching the total number of verses (101) to a name with an equivalent alphabetical value. Tantalizingly, perhaps teasingly, the words "Hugo de" appear near the beginning of *Sir Gawain.* Supposition about authorship has also been based on biographical readings of the poems themselves. Put crudely, the religious nature of *Cleanness* and *Patience* might imply he was a man of the church, and the beautiful and haunting poem *Pearl,* in which a man laments the death of his young daughter, could lead us to think that the author was a bereaved father. On the other hand, he may just as well have been a childless layman with a big imagination and the required amount of religious faith. And it is informed guesswork rather than factual certainty that leads us to suppose that the author was male.

Intriguingly, within *Sir Gawain,* the poet refers to himself in the first person on a number of occasions, as in "I schal telle hit astit, as I in toun herde" (31). Of course, such familiarization between reader and writer is a commonplace literary device, yet it reminds us that somewhere behind the poem is a real person with a story to tell and a gift for telling it. Whether he will ever be named is doubtful, and I for one hope this remains the case, since in my own mind the mystery of his identity and the magic of his poem are quite properly and forever entwined.

About the Translator

Simon Armitage was born in 1963 in the village of Marsden in West Yorkshire. He is a graduate of Portsmouth Polytechnic and Manchester University, and until 1994 worked as Probation Officer in Greater Manchester. His first collection of poems, *Zoom!,* was published in 1989 by Bloodaxe Books, since when there have been a further nine collections, including *Selected Poems* (Faber & Faber 2001), and *Tyrannosaurus Rex Versus the Corduroy Kid* (Faber & Faber 2006). *The Shout—New and Selected Poems* was published in the United States by Harcourt in 2005 and was shortlisted for the National Book Critics Circle Award. He has received numerous awards for his poetry including a Gregory Award, the *Sunday Times* Young Author of the Year, a Forward Prize, and a Lannan Award. With Robert Crawford he edited *The Penguin Anthology of Poetry from Britain and Ireland Since 1945* and edited a selection of Ted Hughes's poetry for Faber & Faber in 2002. He is the author of four stage plays, including *Mister Heracles,* a version of the Euripides play *The Madness of Heracles.* His dramatization of Homer's *Odyssey,* commissioned by the BBC and published by Faber, received the Gold Award at the 2005 Spoken Word Awards. Simon Armitage has written for over a dozen television films. He received an Ivor Novello Award for his song lyrics in the Channel 4 film *Feltham Sings,* which also won a BAFTA, and wrote the libretto for the opera *The Assassin Tree,* composed by Stuart McRae, which premiered at the

Edinburgh International Festival in 2006. His two novels are *Little Green Man* (Penguin 2001) and *The White Stuff* (Penguin 2004). His other prose work includes the best-selling memoir *All Points North* (Penguin 1998), which was the *Yorkshire Post* Book of the Year.

Simon Armitage has taught at the University of Leeds and at the University of Iowa's Writers' Workshop, and is currently a senior lecturer at Manchester Metropolitan University.